# FAIRWAYS
## *of* LIFE

## GOLF WISDOM *of the* LEGENDS

# MATTHEW E. ADAMS

New York Times *best selling author*
AND *PGA Tour Network host*

MORGAN JAMES PUBLISHING • NEW YORK

# FAIRWAYS *of* LIFE

ISBN: 978-1-60037-865-2 (Paperback)
        978-1-60037-866-9 (E-Pub)
Library of Congress Control Number:  2010943202

Published by:
MORGAN JAMES PUBLISHING
1225 Franklin Ave Ste 32
Garden City, NY 11530-1693
Toll Free 800-485-4943
www.MorganJamesPublishing.com

Cover/Interior Design by:
Rachel Lopez
rachel@r2cdesign.com

In an effort to support local communities, raise awareness and funds, Morgan James Publishing donates one percent of all book sales for the life of each book to Habitat for Humanity.
Get involved today, visit **www.HelpHabitatForHumanity.org.**

# DEDICATION

*This book is dedicated to Frank van Doorne and Paul Ferreira,*

*Thank you for your friendship*

# OTHER BOOKS
# BY MATTHEW E. ADAMS

*Chicken Soup for the Soul of America*

*Chicken Soup for the NASCAR Soul*

*Xtreme NASCAR Race Journal for Kids*

*Fast and Lean Racing Cookbook*

*Fairways of Life: Wisdom and Inspiration from the Greatest Game*

*Chicken Soup for the Women Golfer's Soul*

*In the Spirit of the Game*

For more information, contact the author, book a speaking
engagement or place bulk orders, log onto:

## www.FairwaysofLife.com

# TABLE OF CONTENTS

# IN PURSUIT OF PASSION

*ood-bye, for now,* is the way I sign off my show each day. It is a simple phrase, but I have curiously noted that it garners its fair share of attention. This is amusing to me, but the simple reality is that I mean it in the following context: When people care about each other, I do not believe there is a parting, however significant, that is permanent. In other words, "Good-bye," for any duration, is merely temporary, for we shall meet again.

I realize that such a perspective is a mixture of faith, hope and optimism and in that regard, others may view me as naive. So be it. For the most part I believe that the world that surrounds us is the world of our own creation. We have a choice to greet the flow of life's currents with foreboding and lament or we can choose to see adversity as an opportunity to overcome and to succeed. I honestly believe that one makes a choice whether he wishes to dwell in a world of successive failures or conversely, a world that is a series of triumphs (albeit augmented occasionally by temporary setbacks).

It is for this fundamental reason that I believe my life has become immersed in the game of golf, as I have always believed that golf is a game that reflects the very best of human nature.

While I credit my dad with introducing me to the game and nurturing in me a fundamental love and respect for it, it was over twenty-five years ago that I began walking down a path with the game in a capacity beyond an intense hobby. During my summer breaks, I began working at the Lake Waramaug Golf Club, in the foothills of the Berkshire Mountains, not far from where I lived. My experience was not unlike that of millions of others who started at the bottom rungs of the game. Because we were a small club and we had a limited staff, we all did whatever we had to do to get the job done. I did everything from the daily pulling and alignment of the golf carts, to washing dishes in the kitchen or working in the dining room. I learned the "green grass" side of the game literally from the ground up and while the hours were long and the work was intense, they are among my most cherished memories.

Concurrently, and in a theme that continues to define my life today, I also began working in radio (then television) during these formative years. At a young age, I realized that our local AM radio station needed local sports content, which represented an opportunity to cut my teeth. Of course, I had no idea what I was doing, but even as a kid I believed in the philosophy of "biting off more than you can chew," then I would simply chew like crazy. So, in between washing carts or serving hamburgers, at night I would attend local sporting events, interviewing the participants and providing the station with a 30-second "voicer" to wrap up the event. Of course, the radio station could not pay me for my services, but in retrospect, I believe it was I that benefitted the most, as in another recurrent theme of my life, I found a pathway to where I wanted to go in a most non-traditional corridor.

In 1982 (yes, 1982!), I attended my first PGA Tour event as a member of the media as a kid that looked like he was 12 years old (and in reality wasn't much more than that) was credentialed for the Sammy Davis Jr., Greater Hartford Open at the Wethersfield Country Club. While shaking like a leaf, I interviewed celebrities like Bob Hope, Sammy Davis Jr., Jerry Lewis and former President Gerald Ford. It was heady stuff for a mere pup, but I also had the presence of mind (and my father's wise counsel) to realize that media work did not pay a lot, so there was no problem in maintaining my dual career tracks (My media work was a year-round pursuit because in the winter I would focus on my other childhood passion, hockey, so I looked equally out of place during the winter months covering the then, Hartford Whalers, in the NHL.)

This curious mixture of golf, hockey and media work would follow me through my college years where on a weekly basis I would broadcast multiple live collegiate hockey games. In the summer months around the daily duties at the course, I started working on a local cable (television) broadcast of a local golf tournament called *The Greater New Milford Open*, which was run by two dear friends.

It was through these collective efforts that when I graduated from college, ESPN decided to give me a start in the mailroom. Within two months, I was promoted to a PA position in the Production Department where my assignments were the NHL, NFL and SportsCenter. These were mad times of great labor, but even greater learning and they too, are memories that I cherish for in many ways, ESPN was as young as I was in those days.

I left ESPN because the call of the game of golf was just too strong. Within two years of my departure from ESPN, I was hired to work on the golf equipment side of the industry, thus thrusting me down a new, yet oddly related, career path. In this new capacity I learned how and why golf equipment work the way that it does. I worked for a private label production company, which at that time built clubs for RAM, Wilson, MacGregor, Lynx, Nicklaus and Northwestern, among others.

Building and eventually designing golf clubs provided me with one more level of expertise and it was in this capacity that an upstart new cable channel would come to call in the late 1990's, named the Golf Channel. I have never been an employee of the Golf Channel, but have been labeled as a Golf Central "reporter" or "contributor" as the respective roles warranted. In fairness, as of this writing, I do very little with them now other than coverage of the PGA Merchandise Show due to my work hosting a daily show around the world on radio, but I am proud of the work I have done and the exceptional people I have met from there.

Somewhere along this gratuitous career path, opportunity and dexterity crossed paths and I was asked to do some writing for a book called *Chicken Soup for the Golfer's Soul.* While only a ghostwriter, the book became a *New York Times* best seller and the people at *Chicken Soup* kept asking me to do more. Eventually, they asked me to author my own books and after the publication of *Chicken Soup for the Soul of America* and *Chicken Soup for the NASCAR Soul* (providing yet another path of career experience, now in the world of auto racing), soon I was a *New York Times* best selling author in my own right. In the literary world, becoming a *New York Times* best selling author is like winning one of golf's Majors, so now having done it multiple times, it opened up a world of possibilities for me.

Through all of this, I still had golf. Golf, it seems has always been there no matter what direction more superfluous projects might be taking me at any one particular moment. Currently, my dual passions have merged in my covering the PGA Tour for Sirius XM Radio (in North America) and a pursuit I am enjoying as much any other throughout my career. Imagine sharing a love for this great game with a collective audience that feels the same way! How honored I am to have a forum where we can speak with the game's greats while enjoying spirited conversations with listeners from around the world that want to share their experiences with golf. Come Thursday, we broadcast Tour events live and even that is an occasion that causes me to ask myself, "are they really paying me for this?" In between all of this, once the red light goes off, I am back at the golf course (I have a course management company) pulling out golf carts, just like I did when I started in this game. Perhaps we are all destined to retread fundamental elements of our life?

The recounting of all this is not meant to glorify or validate my credentials, but to provide a roadmap for my approach to presenting the game. As I do believe that golf mirrors the human condition, I have compiled the following quotes, stories and anecdotes from a wide variety of sources. Significantly, many of the quotes in this book are unique in that they came from interviews I conducted with the respective subjects, others are well known (and equally classic) quotes from an array of the game's legends, past and present. Finally, this book contains stories, anecdotes (some unique, some I've published previously) and my own perspective garnered from a lifetime around the game and augmented by my experience in the field of literary self-help.

Great champions, whether they are conscious of it or not, seem to impart a nugget of wisdom every time they speak. This book humbly tries to capture some of their inspirational, humorous and thought provoking insights.

I put this book together because golf is foremost, fun. I hope you enjoy this book.

Until we see each other on a golf course, *good-bye, for now*.

*Matt Adams*
February 2011

## CHAPTER 1

# *Passion*

**B**obby Jones could well be the game's ultimate icon. He is renowned for his remaining an amateur (a point of significance that means more from a modern perspective than it was in his day when being a professional golfer did not equate to what it means today) and for accomplishing the game's ultimate feat, winning the "Impregnable Quadrilateral," the Grand Slam, in 1930. This latter feat is looked upon by many as the event that carried Jones up onto the shoulders of public consciousness, but in reality, an incident from five years prior did as much to promote his near mythical legend as anything else he ever did in his legendary career.

By the time of the 1925 U.S. Open at the Worcester Country Club in Worcester, Massachusetts, Bobby Jones was already a superstar with multiple Major victories to his credit. His starring role in the National

Championship was cast alongside of many of the game's reigning powerhouses, including Walter Hagen, Gene Sarazen, Johnny Farrell and Francis Ouimet.

Jones' first round was progressing by conservative measure when he approached his drive in the left rough at the par 4, eleventh hole. Addressing his ball, Jones suddenly backed off. Turning to Walter Hagen, with whom Jones was paired, he declared that his ball had inadvertently moved at address and he intended to assess a penalty stroke as a result, in accordance with the rules of golf. Rules officials weighted in, even surveying members of the gallery to ascertain if anyone had seen the ball moved. Ultimately, a determination outside Jones himself could not be made that any infraction had occurred. Rules officials and Hagen begged Jones to not assess the penalty. Jones would have none of it and he would finish his first round posting a score of 77, well off the pace.

Jones would battle back through oppressively hot and humid weather, with rounds of 70, 70 and 74 to remarkably find himself tied atop the leaderboard at the end of regulation play with Willie MacFarlane, a journeyman professional originally from Carnoustie, Scotland (MacFarlane would post a remarkable score of 67 in the second round). Both golfers would congratulate each other on reaching the playoff that would commence the next morning.

After the morning 18 holes, the two golfers once again found themselves tied. In what was uncharted territory for the USGA, the committee quickly decided that they would play another 18 hole match that afternoon to determine the national champion.

After 35 playoff holes, the two golfers came to the eighteenth hole, still tied. MacFarlane's second shot safely found the top tier of the two-tiered green, leaving him in a safe position to make a par. Knowing that he needed a birdie to win, Jones attempted to hit his approach shot from the right rough, near the front tucked pin. Unfortunately for Jones, his strategy was too aggressive and his shot came to rest in the front bunker. From here, he would hit a remarkable recovery shot to only five feet from the pin, and if he converted that par putt, he would once again be tied with MacFarlane.

But it wasn't to be. To the astonishment of the gallery, Jones missed the crucial putt and the 1925 U.S. Open would belong to Willie MacFarlane by the margin of one stroke.

As a result, Jones' self-assessed one-stroke penalty in the first round took on major significance and would catapult him to a position of national stature.

As Jones possessed mental acuity to match his prowess with a golf club, his passion to adhere to the game's principles (and his own integrity) were illustrated in his post-round comments to the press following the penalty in the first round when after being praised for his honesty, Jones brushed such acclaim aside, countering, "You might as well praise a man for not robbing a bank."

Jones' actions illustrated that passion is an unstoppable force. Passion is not something that is given to us. It is always there, but it sometimes requires that we discover it. Other times we know exactly where our passion lies; we just choose to ignore it. But passion is unrelenting, and refusing to pursue it will not make it go away but will only make us feel frustrated and unfulfilled. Pursue your passion with all your heart.

"You've got to be passionate. You've got to be passionate about life and about business, because if you're not, you've got no right to be trying to run a company because at the end of the day you don't know what you're doing." —**GREG NORMAN**

*"I can sum it up like this—Thank God for the game of golf."* —**ARNOLD PALMER**

"Golf is more in your mind than in your clubs."
—**BRUCE CRAMPTON**

*"It's a great habit to get into."* —**TIGER WOODS**,
after winning his second career Grand Slam

"I can't wait to be in that situation again. I would love to be in it again." —**HUNTER MAHAN**, about being in final singles match of 2010 Ryder Cup against Graeme McDowell

*"I've never felt as nervous on a golf course in my life as I did out there. I mean, trying to do it for my 11 teammates, trying to do it for all these people, trying to do it for Monty, trying to do it for Europe, it's a lot of pressure, it's amazing."* —**GRAEME MCDOWELL**,
after sinking clinching putt, 2010 Ryder Cup

"The constant undying hope for improvement makes golf so exquisitely worth playing."
—**BERNARD DARWIN**

*"I believe I can be the best player in the world."*
—**SUZANN PETTERSEN**

"Golf is the hardest of all sports to play."
—**SAM SNEAD**

*"Champions are never **born**, they are **made**."*
—**MATTHEW E. ADAMS**

"I bought the tractor for my farm. Being a farm boy it was one of my big dreams."
—**LOUIS OOSTHUIZEN**, 2010 Open Champion
about how he spent the prize money

*"I'm so emotional I can barely talk."* —**ANGEL CABRERA**,
after his Masters victory

"It's difficult to excel at something you don't truly enjoy." —**JACK NICKLAUS**

*"Life is not fun unless you're competing."*
—**TIGER WOODS**

"I always dreamed of getting a score like this but didn't think I would do it so fast." —**RYO ISHIKAWA**,
18, after carding a 58 to win The Crowns, a Japan Tour event

*"I've always been a huge golf fan."* —**Peter Jacobsen**

"He's a very clever player and even at 60 years old that still makes him competitive. Playing with him, he made three very smart lay-ups instead of going for greens. But with my length, I find it very difficult not to go for everything even when I am in the rough …It's something I am having to learn."
—**ALVARO QUIROS**, about Tom Watson

*"Dream almost came true."* —**TOM WATSON**,
after 2009 Open Championship

"For me, it's really self-satisfaction. I mean, obviously I feel very good inside when I achieve something that I set out to do. There is no doubt about it. It's the contentment that I get out of it. I mean, I just feel like if I celebrate, or if I treat myself, I have the greatest life. Every day is a great day. If I go out there and achieve something that I want, I just feel really good about it." —**ANNIKA SORENSTAM**

*"So I mean, what's he got going for him? Twenty years of age. Millionaire already. Hits it miles. Nice-looking girlfriend. Drives a Lamborgini. Yeah, it's hard, isn't it?"*
—**LEE WESTWOOD**, about Rory McIlroy

"I've hit a million and a half golf balls in my time, and I've had a plan in my mind for every one of 'em."
—**SAM SNEAD**

*"What other people may find in poetry or art museums, I find in the flight of a good drive."* —**ARNOLD PALMER**

"I'm Zach Johnson and I'm from Cedar Rapids, Iowa." —**ZACH JOHNSON**, addressing the media after his Masters victory

*"You guys see this easy kind of a guy, but I'm a guy that wants to win…"* —**ERNIE ELS**

"When the four-minute mile was first run, the following year I think 55-57 guys ran a four-minute mile." —**PADRAIG HARRINGTON**, 2007, predicting what would happen if a European golfer breaks the 0 for 30 streak in Majors by Europeans (a streak broken by Harrington himself)

*"If you prepare for months and months and set high goals, the last thing to do is be in my own way. There's two people in me; one calm and one totally excited. The calm one won today."* —**ANNIKA SORENSTAM**

"I don't even remember what happened last year. You make a mistake and just put it in the trash."
—**LORENA OCHOA**

*"I think that to score in golf is a matter of confidence, if you think you cannot do it, then there is no chance that you will."* —**HENRY COTTON**

"Golf has been a part of my life all my life."
**—PETER JACOBSEN**

*"There's been a lot of international players who have won, and it made me feel good because, being small in stature, I could go there and win, and these other guys said, 'Listen, if that little runt can do it, I know I can.'"* **—GARY PLAYER**

"First and foremost, you must believe in yourself. You must always pursue quality and have integrity, perseverance and, of course, the desire to succeed."
**—GREG NORMAN**

*"I think at that time I really fell in love with the game. I'd always loved golf, but now it was a new type of love that I could have."* **—TOM WATSON**, after winning the 1977 Open Championship

"I'm very grateful everyday putting on my PGA pin, this was always my dream." **—NATALIE GULBIS**

*"I don't remember anything before golf."* **—RAYMOND FLOYD**

"Keep improving, because I am going to do the same." **—TIGER WOODS**, 2007

*"I didn't know George Washington. But if I did, I would shake his hand and say, 'You're the first, and I won't be the last.'"* **—ARNOLD PALMER**, Congressional Gold Medal recipient. The first was awarded to George Washington in 1776

"Both my love for golf history and golf architecture started in one week when I was 16, when I played the 1968 National Junior in Boston at The Country Club at Brookline." —**BEN CRENSHAW**

*"I hit golf balls from sun up to sun down and by the time I was 13 or 14, I knew exactly what I wanted to be when I grew up."* —**JOHN MAGINESS**, multiple-time winner on Nationwide Tour

"From age 10 or 11, I wanted to be on tour." —**SAM TORRANCE**

"I have such a great passion for the game of golf that it still feels like I was playing high school matches." — **PETER JACOBSEN**

*"Any time you have a problem off the course, you can find sanctuary on it."* —**TIGER WOODS**

"It's a fine line, this game. You're talking one shot a round can be a difference between a good year and a bad year. So it's a very fine line. You know, if you can improve one shot a round, you're four shots over the week; it makes a difference between finishing sixth and first." —**RETIEF GOOSEN**

*"I've made many deals on the golf course."* —**DONALD TRUMP**

"Golf is different then tennis. When you play tennis, you're playing one guy and you're playing the same court." —**LEE TREVINO**

*"The game of golf is fragile and I respect that. I think it's a mirror image on life itself."* —**STEVE STRICKER**

"It's a game we never perfect. Every day it's different. Every track is different." —**LEE TREVINO**

*"Golf has a universal nature."* —**TY VOTAW**

"It's in me it's embedded in my skin." —**TOM KITE**

*"Golf is a very traditional game. I think that anything that is an endeavor in golf has to have sort of a nod to the past."* —**BEN CRENSHAW**

"Golf is such a mental game." —**JOHN MAGINESS**

*"I'm just trying to be more respectful of the game."*
—**TIGER WOODS**

"I think the game of golf is fascinating; it's the mirror of life." —**PETER ALLISS**

## CHAPTER 2

# The Fruits of Labor

## MATTERS OF THE MIND

I t is a matter of public record that Padraig Harrington won over a million dollars at Carnoustie with his 2007 Open Championship victory (Harrington won in a playoff over Sergio Garcia). However, in a move that is nothing short of shocking in today's golf world, Harrington opted to skip the Scottish Open one week earlier, and a potential payday of over one million dollars, when he committed to play in the Irish PGA Championship at the European Club. Potential payday for winning that event: $25,000!

In case you are thinking that Harrington overlooked a couple of decimal points, don't count on it. Harrington was educated as an accountant and his reasons were as planned out as a forensic audit.

The European Club is among Ireland's most challenging links golf course. Harrington reasoned that he would benefit more from a week of competitive links golf experience than he would playing at Loch Lomond, the Tom Weiskopf-designed golf course that, while also challenging and beautiful, is not a links golf course, it's more like an American course. Perhaps on such an American-styled golf course it should not come as a surprise that one of America's biggest golf stars, Phil Mickelson, contended that week. So in the Republic of Ireland, where Padraig Harrington is his country's equivalent to Tiger Woods in popularity, Harrington's entry into the Irish PGA is roughly equivalent to Tiger entering the Massachusetts Open (which actually has a higher purse for first place).

As it turned out, a competitive links experience was what Harrington got, winning the event in sudden-death over Brendan McGovern.

"It definitely helped me. Just getting used to the fact that you could hit 7-iron into the wind and it's only going to go 125 yards. That just doesn't happen in our regular golf. We're used to hitting a 7-iron 180 yards into a slight breeze because it's warm.

All of a sudden you go to a links course and that same little breeze is taking 20, 30 yards off the shot," noted Harrington after The Open. "Today I just worked hard and I think I just drew on all my experience of playing links golf and honestly convinced myself I was going to win."

*"…Convinced myself I was going to win,"* hmmm, interesting, and perhaps another insight into the heart of a champion? I do not think I have ever seen or read about golfers winning a major championship and not found some measure of inspiration in their accomplishment. Almost every victory required some kind of commitment, sacrifice and

often times, the doing of the very thing that everyone else would advise against. Most of all, these champions had an unwavering belief in their abilities, and that, I believe, is the most important attribute of them all.

Jack Nicklaus said that you win major championships with your mind. That could well be the case when one considers that Harrington nearly blew his chances for victory by hitting the wrong club off the tee at 18 (he hit his driver). Yet, through his near Van de Velde-like collapse after hitting his drive into the Barry Burn, and then, incredibly, after taking a penalty drop, hit his next shot into the Burn as well, you would think that he would simply collapse into the fetal position and concede. Yet, he recovered with what he called a "good double-bogey"—and in retrospect, that is exactly what it was, helped in such perspective by Garcia's bogey on the same hole to secure the playoff. Through it all, Harrington's strongest asset was his mind.

"I didn't allow myself to get down about taking six at the last," he revealed. "I convinced myself all along I was going to win and that if it was a playoff, I would do the business."

Golfers including Walter Hagen, Bobby Jones, Ben Hogan, Arnold Palmer, Gary Player, Jack Nicklaus, Lee Trevino, Tom Watson, and Nick Faldo, among others, have all believed that good luck and bad luck come to all golfers in equal measure as does adversity and opportunity.

Champions fight through adversity and take advantage of second chances. They await the fear and pressure to consume the competition around them. The history of Major championships focuses on great shots or fortuitous twists of fate, but Major championships are not won by mere physical forces and luck. Victories are earned through the conviction that success is within their grasp and that their fate is not accountable to any other factor other than the power of their own thoughts.

"Well, I mean, I've always followed the old-timers, Ben Hogan and Gary Player, and they always thought that to get good, you've got to practice. That's the line that I took, and that's what I've always believed in. There's no way up but hard work, and it paid off. The more you do it, the more it pays off, the more important it is to practice. So that's what I did." —**VIJAY SINGH**

*"I wasn't born with this ability. I had to work bloody hard to become the player I am today."* —**COLIN MONTGOMERIE**

"However, looking back on it, I realize that it wasn't as easy as it seemed. There's a lot of work involved. Although it's commented about some of the players how they worked and how many practice balls they may hit, it's probably never really understood how hard they work and what they are doing to get to where they are and to achieve those goals, the sacrifices that are made." —**DAVID DUVAL**

*"Through preparation and hard work, you can prepare yourself for a mental attitude, a zone. When it happens, all you see is the ball and the hole."* —**PAYNE STEWART**

"I always ran scared. I practiced more then anybody." —LEE TREVINO

*"Of course you will continue to have your share of rejections and failures, we all do. Even the best golfers of all time lost 80% of the time they teed it up. But over time, with consistent and persistent effort, you will find that rather than being chastised for your over-the-top-efforts, you will be celebrated for them. The phrase, '**Who does he think he is**?' will soon be replaced with, '**Who else but him**?'"* —MATTHEW E. ADAMS

"I had holes in my game that I needed to rectify in order to be consistent week in and week out. All the great champions that have ever played, that's what they did. I didn't think my game was good enough to come out on tour to do that week in and week out, so I needed to make changes." —TIGER WOODS

*"You've got to love the game. If you don't, you won't work hard enough to make it."* —VAUGHN TAYLOR

"No one has as much luck around the greens as one who practices a lot." —CHI CHI RODRIGUEZ

*"We took it right out of the dirt. We learned to play it our way."* —LEE TREVINO

"I just hung in there. I never gave up, and I just said, I'm going to make a putt sooner or later."—VIJAY SINGH

*"I gave it my all. That's all you can ask for."* —**MIKE WEIR**

"My thing was to play at the highest level."
—**RAYMOND FLOYD**

*"I've got to continue down the path and continue working hard. I want to get to a better level, a higher level, and be more consistent day in and day out. It's as simple as that."*
—**TIGER WOODS**

"I like to get to a tournament and be ready to play, do all my work outside, and when I come here I'm ready to go." —**VIJAY SINGH**

*"One of the things that makes the game of golf so unique is that professional golfers are **independent contractors**. Play well, you get paid. Miss the cut, and you get nothing. I cannot think of a situation that is more reflective of a free market than that. Aside from endorsement contracts (that come after some level of accomplishment and will quickly vanish if the golfer does not continue to perform), professional golfers are paid based upon what they earn, just like you and me, and in that regard we are all **independent contractors**, even if we work for someone else. Once we embrace this concept we start to become accountable to ourselves for our level and quality of productivity. Questions like, **How much money do we want to make?** or **How do we want to be perceived by co-workers and competitors?** become variables within*

*our grasp based upon how hard we are willing to work and how much time and energy we are willing to invest in our personal product, service and reputation. The best thing about an **independent contractor** mentality is that it liberates you from the insecurity of relying upon the opinion of others as to our true capacity. Will we make the cut, or will we aspire to be champions? It is our choice."* —**MATTHEW E. ADAMS**

"I worked as hard to perfect my golf game as any other fellow would work in his brokerage office, in his job as a mechanic in a garage, as a lawyer or as a traveling salesman." —**WALTER HAGEN**

*"The first thing I always tell young people is that I never dissipated. I didn't drink, I didn't smoke, I didn't chase women and I always exercised. I was always active and I thought right. I wanted to do things that made people proud of what they were."* —**BYRON NELSON** in 2006 at age 94

"Confidence comes from getting started."
—**LEE TREVINO**

*"At 75 I still do 1,000 sit ups almost every day."*
—**GARY PLAYER**

"I pursue it 100% when I pursue it."
—**RAYMOND FLOYD**

*"The biggest expectation comes from me."* —**STEVE STRICKER**

"I just played, and I played my heart out."
—**LEE TREVINO**

*"You need exercise and hard work;
you can't just take a pill."* —**GARY PLAYER**

"It's not about fear it's about diligence."
—**VAL SKINNER**

*"I'm a competitor first and I play golf."* —**TOM KITE**

"Preparing and working hard, there's really no
substitute for those kinds of things and they usually
pay pretty good dividends." —**DAVE ADAMONIS, SR.**

*"Physical ability is not the only tool that is needed. I think
you have to have a mental toughness."* —**RAYMOND FLOYD**

"Good habits are formed if you keep relying on
yourself and the way you can play." —**BEN CRENSHAW**

*"It was a tough road and it took a long time to get there."*
—**JOHN MAGINESS**

"It takes four wins. Everything has to come together
at the right time, the moon and stars, and there
is a lot of luck involved." —**TIGER WOODS**,
on what it takes to win the Grand Slam

*"Practice puts brains in your muscles."* —**SAM SNEAD**

"There is nothing in this game of golf that
can't be improved upon if you practice."
—**PATTY BERG**

*"Champions control the violence within themselves."*
**—BOB TOSKI**

"Everyone is pretty optimistic. You've got goals,
New Year's resolutions, things you want to achieve.
If you're not optimistic this time of the year,
I'd sure as hell hate to see what your attitude
is like in October." **—JIM FURYK**,

discussing his mindset at the beginning of 2011

*"The strengths of my game were developed in the States. As a
student, I found the weather and the facilities were so good
that I wanted to practice seven days a week. I put in a hell-
of-a-lot of effort in college. I wasn't born with this ability. I
had to work bloody hard to become the player I am today."*
**—COLIN MONTGOMERIE**

"My formula for success is simple: practice
and concentration; then more practice and
concentration." **—BABE ZAHARIAS**

*"Those are the same clubs I used last week. Last week I'm
shooting 80 this week 70."* **—LEE TREVINO**

## CHAPTER 3

# *Perspective*

"*If you're out there…go.*"

From out of the ether, somewhere lost in the sea of clatter in a broadcaster's headset, my still nameless, faceless producer had launched my most prominent golf broadcasting experience to date.

"*You're looking live at the famed Road Hole at the Old Course of St Andrews in the first round of the 150th Anniversary of the Open Championship.*" I played my verbal approach safely down the middle.

I did not set out for this Open Championship knowing that I would have anything to do with ESPN's massive efforts to bring the sights and sounds of the 2010 Open to the eager eyes of golf fans around the world, it just seemed to work out that way, although the route I did take was entertaining enough.

I met one of my best friends, Paul Ferreira, at the airport, the first step in our golfing odyssey. Paulie only lives about forty minutes from me, but such as life's currents flow, we rarely see each other unless we are traveling to some far-flung part of the world in search of golfing adventure. This edition would see us flying from Boston, through London's Heathrow, on to Amsterdam. After the wheels touched down in Holland, we met up with another of our best friends, Frank van Doorne, who greeted us at the baggage claim. Frank was eager to show us his homeland and proceeded to whisk us through the Netherlands, destined for a new Colin Montgomerie designed golf development appropriately called The Dutch (where Frank is one of the founding members), wherefrom I would broadcast my live, two-hour radio show on the PGA Tour Network, heard on SiriusXM Radio in North America.

Thanks to Paul's Mr. Scott-like ability to pull together a global satellite broadcast from a pile of smoldering wires (in an illustration of my technology impairment, somehow I plugged my mixing board into the wrong outlet and my mixer expired in a cloud of black smoke), the show from The Dutch went well and we were treated to a tour of the still-under-construction course and were implored to come back when it opened the following year (an invitation I intend to take advantage of).

From there, Frank treated us to a round of golf and fellowship on his Harry Colt designed home course, Eindhoven Golf Club (which was awesome). Following the golf, dinner and craic ("good times" in native Irish), we met up with Frank's friends Maarten and Stephanie to take in the nightlife of Eindhoven. Bearing in mind that this was the night before the finals of the World Cup, in which Holland was to meet Spain, the mood was, to say the least, festive and quickly became wild. After enjoying the sights and sounds of the plaza, Frank guided us to an Irish pub (no doubt, to make me feel at home). The pub was packed with revelers, all shoulder to shoulder, drenched in summer sweat and Guinness and with an assortment of summer footwear and flip-flops sticking to the glazed slate floor. Suddenly, the pub door burst open and from the haze of a summer shower jumped a shirtless, hairy man wildly wielding a screaming chainsaw!

My friends Paulie and Maarten bravely jumped behind me, marking me as the first victim of the jaws of the vicious saw. Armed with only my pint of Guinness, which I would not sacrifice even for the price of a limb or two, I weighed my options…there were none. Thankfully, the shirtless, hairy madman apparently grew weary of swinging the angry saw back and forth and when its slashing rhythm had slowed, I could see that the saw was without its teeth, the chain having been removed. This revelation either settled on the entirety of the pub already, or the practice of sacrificing an Irishman to the spinning blades is something of a nightly occurrence. Either due to the pace of the events or the aforementioned Guinness, I never did get an answer.

Night abruptly became morn and we were on our way back to Amsterdam and then on to Edinburgh, Scotland. Soon we were dropping off our bags in the dorm rooms we reserved at St Andrews University, feeling very much as if we had just checked into Hogwarts. The day's travels flew by in the same manner as my recollections of the evening prior (a haze). Before we knew it, we were huddled away in the Scores basement pub in St Andrews, less than 100 yards from the first tee of the famed grand lady. Even without a dog in the race, the Scots came out in force to watch the World Cup, so Frank was nervous that he would miss his countrymen's efforts due to lack of space at the pub. Luckily, we found three empty stools at a table where two men were already sitting. Pleasantries were exchanged and a conversation ensued, each party sharing why they were sitting on the doorstep of the 150th anniversary of the world's oldest Major. As it were, our table company, Don Colantonio and Brian Williams were the Sr. Director Interactive TV and Producer/Director, respectively, of the ESPN Experience on Direct TV. Don asked that if my duties with the PGA Tour Network did not consume all of my time, might I be willing to fill in on his broadcast? The answer, of course, was an emphatic yes!

The next few days were spent walking every inch of the Old Course (including the obligatory jaunt across the Swilken Bridge!) and watching the best golfers in the world practice, reacquainting ourselves with the "Auld grey toon," and broadcasting my show live from the Media Centre, alongside the first hole. When the schedule permitted, we even snuck away to Kingsbarns (absolutely world-class), part of the rotation along with the Old Course and Carnoustie (which we also played) for the European Tour's Dunhill Links, benefitted in the evenings by the fact that the sun doesn't set until past 10 pm. Due to the time zone and our agenda, our day's work at the Media Centre usually wrapped up around 11 pm, where after a quick Macallan at the Scores pub, we would set off across the sleeping Old Course to our waiting car (guided by an ethereally lit R & A building) and soon we were off to a blissful slumber. Throughout the week and more often then not, Frank, Pauly and I would share looks of wonderment that silently screamed, "Can you believe this!"

The day before the start of the tournament proper, a gale blew in off the North Sea that was as vicious a storm as I've seen. Sadly, as a result, the Champions Challenge that was scheduled to include past champions Lee Trevino, Tony Jacklin, Greg Norman, Mark Calcavecchia and John Daly, among others, was cancelled due to the weather.

The dawn of the opening day of the tournament brought with it an easier work load because my network was carrying the live worldwide coverage of the Open Championship provided by Radio Open Golf, so my regular show did not air. After doing some hits with the Radio Open crew, we set off for the ESPN tower. What a magnificent sight it was to behold. Three stories high, it was tucked along the right side of the first fairway, in front of the burn and just behind the second tee. From our perch we had a fabulous and unobstructed view of the entire first hole, eighteenth hole, the Road Hole's bunker and green complex and the second tee. My job was to host the coverage at specific holes, either the Road Hole, first hole or eighteenth hole. My first assignment was the Road Hole and I was in nothing short of golf heaven.

The story of Louis Oosthuizen's glorious march to victory ultimately defined this Open and when it was all said and done, I had broadcast sixteen hours of live coverage on SiriusXM Radio (guided and aided by the talents of Frank, Paulie, my producers Jeremy Davis, Justin Ware and Dominic Scarano and co-host Fred Albers) and eleven hours of live coverage for ESPN! I know that in today's world it is a rare opportunity when one feels honored to do a job that he is also paid for, but this dichotomy very much defined my emotions at St Andrews (not that I would not have happily done it for free).

*"If you're out there…go,"* were the sage words of my producer Jim LePera. I can think of no better a philosophy to live by.

"You don't ever want to try to win, try to force a win. That never happens. You just take it as a process. It's 72 holes. You take it a shot at a time and hopefully at the end of the week, you're on top. You never ever try to force a win." —**TIGER WOODS**

*"Not every missed putt is due to a deep psychological insecurity. Complete conviction and solid execution on the wrong line, regardless of your level of confidence, will not a putt make. However, more short putts, both on and off the golf course, have been missed due to a lack of conviction than those lipped out by poor judgment."* —**MATTHEW E. ADAMS**

"Pain and suffering are inevitable in our lives, but misery is an option." —**CHIP BECK**

*"Give luck a chance to happen."* —**TOM KITE**

"Visualize winning." —**GARY PLAYER**

*"Always keep learning. It keeps you young."* —**PATTY BERG**

"You can think best when you're happiest."
—**PETER THOMSON**

*"That's what I work on probably more than anything. I love to chip and I love to putt. In golf today, kids even, they want to go on the driving range and just beat balls*

*and beat balls. The outings and stuff I do all over the country and the world, all you see is kids on the driving range. You never see them chipping and putting that much, and that's something that I think the Tour, all of the players, we need to look hard at and help grow the game. We've got to get better at that."* —**JOHN DALY**

"How much time are you spending on the three-foot putts in your life? How often do you overtly or subconsciously prequalify yourself for failure?
'She would never go out on a date with someone like me.'
'I can't apply for that job; they'd never hire me.'
'I can't make this putt. I always miss them.'
'I just can't beat this guy.'
These self-defeating prophecies are destined to become reality because to do nothing, to choose the path of least resistance, to accept failure, is easy. In fact, you will likely be comforted by your supporters with clichés like, 'It's not what you know, but who you know.'
Do not accept this. Get to know the right people. Fight through the compulsion to accept mediocrity." —**MATTHEW E. ADAMS**

*"First of all, you only get out of it what you put into it. If you are a sheep in this world, you're not going to get much out of it. You can't be a sheep in golf. You have to strive to be the best. To be the best, you have to be a leader. And to be a leader, you have to be a leader to yourself."* —**GREG NORMAN**

"I could take out of my life everything
except my experiences at St Andrews and
I'd still have a rich, full life." —**BOBBY JONES**

*"The guy who believes in happy endings is going to play
consistently better golf than the man who approaches every
act of existence with fear and foreboding."* —**TONY LEMA**

"A kid grows up faster on the golf course. Golf
teaches you how to behave." —**JACK NICKLAUS**

*"I was lucky to win. I've never been happier to get any cup,
and I never worked so hard nor suffered so much, either."*
—**BOBBY JONES**, on his 1930 British Amateur victory

"If I happen to start out with four fives, I simply
figure that I've used up my quota. I forget them and
start out on a new track." —**WALTER HAGEN**

*"If you have your game on, it doesn't matter what golf
course you play."* —**TIGER WOODS**

"The biggest thing is to have the mindset and belief
that you can win every tournament. Nicklaus had it."
—**TIGER WOODS**

*"Everyone has both 'good' and 'bad' luck every day. It is
amazing that the golfer who does not complain or dwell
on the occurrence of bad luck is assumed to not have any,
while the one who bemoans his fate is assumed to have*

*nothing but bad luck. The latter is a limiting mentality that leads to self-defeat."* —**MATTHEW E. ADAMS**

"The first thing anybody has to do to be any good at anything is believe in himself." —**GAY BREWER**

*"No one remembers who came in second."* —**WALTER HAGEN**

"I'm a lucky dog. You got to be lucky to beat Jack Nicklaus, because he's the greatest golfer who ever held a club." —**LEE TREVINO**, after defeating Nicklaus in a playoff at the 1971 U.S. Open

*"You win major tournaments with your mind."*
—**TIGER WOODS**

"If you put yourself there enough times, you're going to win your share." —**TIGER WOODS**

*"One always feels that he is running from something without knowing what nor where it is."*
—**BOBBY JONES**, on pressure in Majors

"I came to the tournament with nothing to lose, and that had everything to do with winning."
—**JOHN DALY**, 1991 PGA Champion

*"What made America a great country was people coming from all over the world and working their butts off."*
—**GARY PLAYER**

"I go into the locker room and find a corner and just sit there. I try to achieve a peaceful state of nothingness that will carry over onto the golf course. If I can get that feeling of quiet and obliviousness within myself, I feel I can't lose." —**JANE BLALOCK**

*"If there is a fountain of youth, it has to be exercise."*
—**GARY PLAYER**

"I've heard players speak proudly of fifth-place finishes. If you can be happy with fifth, it could be that you don't have what it takes to win." —**MICKEY WRIGHT**

*"I cling to a few tattered old virtues, like believing that you don't get anything in this world for nothing."*—**TONY LEMA**

"It is difficult to describe why the addicting game of golf is so endearing. I believe it is because the game allows us a glimpse of perfection. How often have you endured a horrible round, replete with proclamations of quitting the game, only to be saved by that one miraculous shot that keeps you coming back?" —**MATTHEW E. ADAMS**

*"You don't necessarily have to be a good golfer to be a good putter, but you have to be a good putter to be a good golfer."*—**TONY LEMA**

"Most people live their lives chained to the oars of a life of their own making whether defined by one's job, relationships, self-image, or golf game. More often then not, the biggest obstacles we face in life are those that we have placed in our own path."
—**MATTHEW E. ADAMS**

*"The Lord hates a coward."* —**BYRON NELSON**

"You've got to be good at losing, if you're going to be a good winner. And I feel like I'm great at losing, but I also feel like I'm great at winning. I think a guy that loses well is going to win a lot more than guys that don't lose well." —**DARREN CLARKE**

*"The difference between winning and losing is always a mental one."* —**PETER THOMSON**

"It nauseated me. I could vomit when I see one. It's like a rattlesnake in your pocket." —**BEN HOGAN**, on a hook

*"Any time you are in a final pairing it's fun, but I tell you, it's even more fun winning in that final pairing in a major championship. That's why you play, why you practice, that's why you dream as a kid, and that's why you put in all of those long hours."* —**TIGER WOODS**

"The older you get, the less you realize you know. It's the same way with golf. You get out here long enough, you realize, 'Wow, it is really hard to win.' But maybe that's another reason why I've only won twice." —**PAUL GOYDOS**

*"It seems to me to be a logical way in which to influence our children, if for no other reason than they have to sort of do it themselves. They have to learn some independence, they have to learn some integrity, they have to learn how to play with rules, and I think those are issues that sort of get lost in the shuffle nowadays."* —**HALE IRWIN**, about golf

"A good golfer has the determination to win and the patience to wait for the breaks." —**GARY PLAYER**

*"Some people think they are concentrating when they are merely worrying."* —**BOBBY JONES**

"I think it's just that you, you just have a confidence about you and with that confidence it frees everything up, it frees your swing up, it frees your mind up and you just seem to be, you just ride the wave. It is like getting on top of the wave and you ride it as long as you can stay up on top of the wave." —**PAYNE STEWART**

*"I think you have to really, really want to do it before it's going to happen."* —**DAVID TOMS**

"You can practice yourself into self doubt if you're not careful. So if it's good, and I'm a classic case of, if it's not busted, no way I'm going to fix anything, you know, just leave it the way it is."
—**COLIN MONTGOMERIE**

*"It's the Ryder Cup. It's what it does to your heart."*
**—SAM TORRANCE**

"Getting better comes from within. This is a game that's fluid, it's always changing. It's always evolving, and every facet of the game can always improve."
**—TIGER WOODS**

*"What happens is people give up too early."* **—LEE TREVINO**

"The ones that sell the most balls are the ones that advertise the best." **—GARY PLAYER**

*"If you think of yourself as unlucky, you'll have bad luck. The second you start thinking of yourself as a victim, you've had it."* **—TOM WATSON**

"Years from now, people may remember me as a golfer and a major champion. But I'd like also to be remembered as somebody who took the issue of autism and did something with it." **—ERNIE ELS**, 2011

*"When you're putting good, the swing doesn't matter because you feel like you can get it up and down from anywhere. If I can get the putter worked out, I think I'll be alright."* **—BILL HAAS**

## CHAPTER 4

# A Beautiful Walk

## A Spectator at the Crossroads of History

Long before the dramatic events of November of that year, the 2009 Memorial tournament will be remembered for Tiger Woods' heroics on the final day of the competition. Tiger Woods did, of course, what Tiger Woods has historically done, erasing a four shot deficit at the start of the day and winning the event in dramatic fashion by making birdies on the finishing holes, including a virtual tap-in for birdie at the difficult 18th hole, to secure the victory (by one stroke over Jim Furyk). I was there as part of the PGA Tour Network's live coverage crew (I was assigned to do the on course play-by-play for Tiger Woods for both Thursday's and Saturday's rounds), but the events of the week that left the greatest impression on me took place the Wednesday before the first round.

On that day, Jack Nicklaus, Tiger Woods and six other Tour stars got together for the first ever Memorial Skins game, for charity. Mr. Nicklaus and Tiger were paired together. With no disrespect intended to the other six golfers involved, it might as well have been just Mr. Nicklaus and Tiger on the course, for the focus of everyone was singular.

Somehow it seemed that fate itself was conspiring against the occasion. The weather in Ohio, was in a word, awful. Breezy, with temperatures barely cracking fifty degrees, and the ultimate indignity, the teeming down rain that accompanied the nine-hole exhibition.

But one thing was for certain. In a world where history usually chooses to define itself at a moment that suits its means, there in Dublin, Ohio—an Irish inspired city name, on Muirfield Village—a Scottish inspired name that was a reflection of Mr. Nicklaus' love for one of the great golf courses in the world, in the most Celtic of weather, history would meet at a crossroads and me and my 5,000 or so fellow drowned rats were treated to watching two of the greatest golfers of all time play side by side.

My credentials allowed me inside the ropes and I walked along, usually only a few feet from the competitors. I could hear their banter as they went along and honestly, it was not remarkable. There were no philosophical discussions about their place(s) in golf's history books or the significance of the historical bridges their walking side-by-side represented. Instead, it was usually discussions about how far it was to clear this bunker or hazard (usually 270 or 290 yards), with Mr.

Nicklaus good-naturally chiming in "you weren't telling that to me, were you?" At one point, Tiger hit his approach shot on the par 5, 11th hole, wayward to the right and as he walked over, he asked me if I saw where it went. I pointed to my right, in a batch of large trees. As he passed, Woods smiled and said to no one in particular, "it's supposed to bounce out" (he nearly birdied the hole anyway).

For the record, and while it was not official, Jack Nicklaus appeared to be hitting his driver about 270 yards that day and was for the most part, 30 yards behind his fellow competitors, conceding about 21 years to the oldest, Kenny Perry, who was 48. Ever the competitor, Mr. Nicklaus won two skins that day. The overall winner, you guessed it, was Tiger Woods, after making an impossible chip-in at the 18th Hole, in a playoff.

The debate will continue to rage as to who is the greatest golfer of all time (I am of the belief that it is Jack Nicklaus, until such time as, and if, his place atop the record books is supplanted), but on this special day, it was not about who is better, it was about one of the rarest sightings in all of sport, it was about watching 32 combined professional Major victories walk down the fairways together in a rain shrouded forum that only the game of golf could provide.

"The game is meant to be fun." —**JACK NICKLAUS**

*"You never get to where you want to be. That's the beautiful thing about the game, because tomorrow can always be better."* —**TIGER WOODS**

"That's all I play for, to win and compete
and be in the top. I don't play for the money,
I just play because I love the game of golf and
I love working on my game." —**JULIE INKSTER**

*"I love the game. I love the competition. And golf
is my life. Thanks to golf, I have what I have and
what I have achieved and I'm very grateful to the game."*
—**SEVE BALLESTEROS**

"Golf is a game of finding what works, losing it,
and finding it again." —**KEN VENTURI**

*"Enjoy the game. Happy golf is good golf."* —**GARY PLAYER**

"The quicker you can realize that golf is not everything,
the better your golf will probably be because you
take your mind off of it." —**GREG NORMAN**

*"Yes, golf has been my savior, there is no doubt about it."*
—**ANNIKA SORENSTAM**

"I think it's a great game, I enjoy to compete, I
enjoy the competition and just to be out here and
be able to play, its fantastic." —**SEVE BALLESTEROS**

*"Golf is a game in which you try to put a small ball
in a small hole with implements singularly unsuited
to the purpose."* —**WINSTON CHURCHILL**

"Playing golf is like eating. It's something which has to come naturally." —**SAM SNEAD**

*"Playing golf isn't any fun if you're not having fun playing."* —**JOYCE WETHERED**

"This is the essence of strategic architecture: to encourage initiative, reward a well-played stroke, and yet to insist that there must be planning and honest self-appraisal behind the daring."
—**ROBERT TRENT JONES, SR.**

*"Golf is a job to me. I love to play, but I'm very serious about what I do."* —**VIJAY SINGH**

"Go out and have fun. Golf is a game for everyone, not just for the talented few." —**HARVEY PENICK**

*"Golf is twenty percent mechanics and technique. The other eighty percent is philosophy, humor, tragedy, romance, melodrama, companionship, camaraderie, cussedness and conversation."* —**GRANTLAND RICE**

"I get to play golf for a living. What more can you ask for—getting paid for doing what you love."
—**TIGER WOODS**

*"Golf is a game of integrity."* —**RAY FLOYD**

"Golf is like solitaire. When you cheat,
you only cheat yourself." —**TONY LEMA**

*"Yes, as golf is a human game, mistakes will happen.
Being able to laugh at a situation will open the
opportunity to learn from it without our minds becoming
shut down through rage."* —**MATTHEW E. ADAMS**

"I learn something new about the game almost
every time I step on the course." —**BEN HOGAN**

*"Respect. The game of golf is based on etiquette and respect.
I grew up with it, Jack grew up with it, Arnold (Palmer)
grew up with it. Jack and Arnold and Gary have always
been great models of etiquette on the golf course and the way
the game should be played. It's a lot different game in other
sports, where the respect which used to be there is not shown
so much anymore. It's disheartening to see it sometimes
in other sports, but golf, it's remained pretty constant and
that's the beauty of the game."* —**TOM WATSON**

"I think it's the beauty of the courses, the beauty of
the walk. I've made many great friends and some
enemies on the golf course." —**DONALD TRUMP**

*"I used golf as my beacon of hope. It's golf that kept me going."*
—**KEN GREEN**, after his horrific car accident and the loss of his son

"I don't think it matters how good you are or what ranking in the world, or how many tournaments you've won; I think you should always try to get better because golf is a game you cannot perfect."

—**SAM SAUNDERS**, professional golfer and grandson of Arnold Palmer on what he has learned from his grandfather

*"I enjoy the game and I enjoy my friends. That is something very important to me."* —**ARNOLD PALMER**

"I would have given all the money back just for the experience, the education."

—**LEE TREVINO**, on what the game has meant to him

*"There was nothing in my life I liked more at that time then golf; nothing was even a close substitute."* —**TONY JACKLIN**

"It's nice to feel part of something." —**CHRIS DIMARCO**

*"Golf is a great sport that brings together a lot of different audiences."* —**NATALIE GULBIS**

"You got to have fun. It's still just a game." —**TOM KITE**

*"I want to be a part of what's right about the game of golf."* —**PETER JACOBSEN**

"Golf is fantastic. I love the game so much! I love the game so much! I love the game so much!"

—**BOO WEEKLY**

*"Golf is usually played with the outward appearance of great dignity. It is, nevertheless, a game of considerable passion, either of the explosive type or that which burns inwardly."* —**BOBBY JONES**

"Golf is a compromise between what your ego wants you to do, what experience tells you to do, and what your nerves will let you do." —**BRUCE CRAMPTON**

*"Golf is deceptively simple, yet endlessly complicated."* —**ARNOLD PALMER**

"I enjoy playing golf, I really do. In some strange way, although I had not played much in the last 18 months or so, it's been some of the more enjoyable times because it just goes to show you how hard the game can be. And you know, it makes you appreciate the skills the players have and the things they work on, the things they do because it's just a very, very hard game." —**DAVID DUVAL**

*"Golf is like driving a car. As you get older, you get more careful."* —**SAM SNEAD**

"It's a game of adjustments, a game of constant change and adjustment." —**BEN HOGAN**

*"Putting is like wisdom—partly a natural gift and partly the accumulation of experience."* —**ARNOLD PALMER**

"It's the beauty of this game, it's a humbling endeavor. It's one you'll never perfect, but that's what intrigues me and that's why I keep working."
—**TOM KITE**

*"You're not going to totally master this game. As good as Tiger Woods is, he's never going to master this game. He's better than most of the guys out there, but at the end of the day, you know, golf is golf."* —**ERNIE ELS**

"There are social aspects of the game and I think people overlook that" —**PETER JACOBSEN**

*"You're never too old to play golf.*
*If you can walk, you can play."* —**LOUISE SUGGS**

"The thing that sets golf apart from other sports is that it takes self-confidence, an ability to rely totally on yourself." —**JACK NICKLAUS**

*"Golf is good for the soul. You get so mad at yourself you forget to hate your enemies."* —**WILL ROGERS**

"The game of golf has a way of divulging aspects of our character that we would probably prefer were left hidden, sometimes even from ourselves."
—**MATTHEW E. ADAMS**

*"Playing golf isn't any fun if you're not having fun playing."*
—**JOYCE WETHERED**

"I think as much as anything else, it's a silly old game. All we are doing is playing a game." —**DAVID DUVAL**

*"Golf is the hardest game in the world. There is no way you can ever get it. Just when you think you do, the game jumps up and puts you in your place."* —**BEN CRENSHAW**

"No one will ever have golf under his thumb. No round ever will be so good it could not have been better. Perhaps this is why golf is the greatest of games." —**BOBBY JONES**

*"Golf is a game that mirrors life. Golf is both a mystical journey of joy and sorrow and a physical journey of cause and effect. It is a game providing us with opportunities for wonderfully torturous choices—take a chance and achieve supreme glory or wallow in dismal failure— always with the promise of another day to try again."*
—**MATTHEW E. ADAMS**

"Golf is a game of precision, not strength."
—**JACK NICKLAUS**

*"Golf is my job and motivates me... It's a very complex game, very challenging. You never stop learning."*
—**BETSY KING**

"Golf is not a game of great shots. It's a game of the most misses. The people who win make the smallest mistakes." —**GENE LITTLER**

*"Golf is in the interest of good health and good manners.*
*It promotes self interest and affords a chance to*
*play the man and act the gentleman."*
**—PRESIDENT WILLIAM HOWARD TAFT**

## CHAPTER 5

# *The Driving Force:*
## *Dad, Family and Inspirations*

### PLAY HAPPY

I s one's path to greatness usually paved with smooth, clear lines of access, training and success, or are the truly great ones a product of overcoming the obstacles in their path? Obstacles that would otherwise stop all others?

Such was the mental posture with which I approached the story of Nancy Lopez and her seemingly meteoric ascent to fame. I will admit that I was expecting to be regaled with stories of a childhood full of privilege and luxury. Of lazy summer days spent by the country club pool and afternoons strolling the manicured lawn called a golf course, where some latent golfing talent would reveal itself and define a golfing prodigy. Surely, it would have to be a person of deep golf heritage and a life literally growing up around the game to create so massive a star at such a young age?

In the story of Nancy Lopez and the vision and impact of her father, Domingo, I found my preconceived notions dispelled.

Nancy Lopez was not born into a life of privilege. She was born in 1957 to a Mexican-American family of modest means. Lopez learned to golf from her father, Domingo. Domingo owned a local auto repair shop in Roswell, N.M., the town where Nancy grew up. He believed in his heart that his daughter would one day be famous and he and his wife, Maria, would scrimp and scrape together whatever they could to help their daughter succeed. He gave Nancy her first golf club, a sawed off fairway wood, when she was eight years old. The family could not afford golf lessons so Domingo would be her teacher.

Experts will assert that Nancy Lopez has an unorthodox swing and maybe they are right. Then again, didn't they say the same thing about Arnold Palmer and Lee Trevino?

Perhaps Domingo did not give his daughter a picture-perfect golf swing but he did give her a few gems that would prove to be like a suit of armor in the heat of competition. Domingo taught his daughter to *"play happy."*

Today, it is common to see teenage golfers who wear a scowl like a badge of honor. At what point was it determined that if you do not spend half your day on the golf course lamenting your inadequacies, then you just were not trying hard enough? Are these the virtues we are instilling in our children? Not to Domingo. He taught Nancy that attitude was as important as technical performance. That golf is a thinking-person's game and that the eventual winner is likely not the one with superior technical ability, but the one who has the mental fortitude to not tighten up under pressure. This is a powerful lesson whether one is putting for the win or trying to keep one's sanity in rush-hour traffic, with a kid to pick up at soccer practice, or a trying to fit a week's worth of work into a 24-hour day.

Domingo also gave his daughter the right to believe in herself. He was so convinced of her abilities that he allowed his convictions and confidence to permeate his daughter's psyche. I found this to be another powerfully simple concept; to celebrate your child's unique strengths and gifts rather than constantly harping on his or her weaknesses.

Nancy Lopez soon began to deliver on the promise of her talents. At 12 years-old she won the New Mexico Amateur. As a teen, she won the U.S.G.A. Junior Girls Championship twice. At 18, she remarkably finished second in the U.S. Open. She led her high school golf team to two state titles. It serves to be mentioned that her high school golf team was otherwise comprised of all men. She went on to earn a college scholarship at Tulsa (the first women to receive a full scholarship there) and in her freshmen year she was an All-American and Tulsa's Female Athlete of the Year. Lopez would turn professional at the end of her sophomore year, in 1977.

Lopez had a strong start to her first professional season, but later that year, she would lose her beloved mother after complications from surgery. As can be expected, the loss of her mother had a profound effect on such a young woman. But, with the heart of a champion, she would channel her emotions with laser-like focus. She has called this time the turning point of her life and that which made her more mentally strong. In 26 tournaments in 1978, Lopez won nine times, including a stretch of five straight victories and a six stroke win at the LPGA Championship. The next year, she would repeat as the Player-of-the-Year, in addition to another eight championships. Lopez would continue her solid play until she had to cut back on her playing time in 1983 due to the birth of her first child. She would end up with three girls, and in 2002, she announced that she would no longer be maintaining a full playing schedule in order to spend more time with her family.

Lopez, who was inducted into the Hall of Fame at only 30 years old, would end her full-time playing career having won a total of 48 championships (she would win her last tournament in 1997), and in 2000, she was recognized as one of the LPGA's Top 50 Players of All Time. Through all of this success, she continues to "play happy," infecting everyone with her warmth and charisma.

Life has a way of making us feel overwhelmed, but in the story of Nancy Lopez's life I found inspiration from a father who chose to empower his daughter with possibilities.

"I worked myself to a point where I said, 'There's nothing else going to come between me and my goal.' That was it. I had a lot of support. My team was great. My trainer, Joey, my wife, my caddie. Everything worked out fine. I think you need a good team behind you to have a successful year, and I did."
**—VIJAY SINGH**

*"There are times I could have gone down the wrong path, but dad was always there."* **—TIGER WOODS**

"My dad taught me that I was not the only person to inhabit the earth, and that I should treat everyone with the same respect and dignity with which I hoped they would treat me. He taught me the value of hard work, commitment, dedication, and loyalty. He helped me to see that no man stands alone, and that the day you start to believe that you are better than your fellow man, well, then I guess you truly are alone."
—**ARNOLD PALMER**, from the Foreword of Fairways of Life

*"I mean, he's my dad and I love him to death. He's my best friend, and any time you can spend as much time with your parents that you truly love, especially when he wasn't feeling all that well, it meant the world to me."* —**TIGER WOODS**

"I started golf at eight. Dad had an auto body repair shop. He and mom sacrificed all the time. Every extra cent was used to get me into amateur tournaments. They gave up things to make sure I had clothes that looked nice. They would go without, so I could have three new balls or new socks. My wonderful parents gave me the opportunity to compete with the best and get the experience I needed to be successful."
—**NANCY LOPEZ**

*"My dad is my ultimate guru."* —**ERNIE ELS**

"Trust me, it's not always easy, but my father has always harped on me, always be honest with yourself, true to yourself, look yourself in the mirror and be honest. Some days are tougher than others. When you know you've absolutely messed up, you have to admit it and move on and learn and apply." —**TIGER WOODS**

*"My father taught me that golf is like a lifelong love affair.
It begins with an infatuation, develops into a senseless love,
and matures into a contentious, maddening, frustrating,
exhilarating, fulfilling, and yet understanding kind of bond you
see in an elderly couple in the park."* —**MATTHEW E. ADAMS**

"I motivate myself by thinking of my family. If I can't be with them at home, I'd rather make my time out here worthwhile. If I play well, I feel like I can justify being away from them; it's OK to leave them that week. If I don't play well, then I feel like I've wasted time I could have spent with them." —**NANCY LOPEZ**

*"The most important thing he did for me was
give me a positive attitude about my abilities."*
—**TOM WATSON**, about Byron Nelson

"Mom was the one I was always afraid of. Yeah, you have no idea how competitive my mom is. She would watch me compete living every moment, live [and] I mean die on every shot." —**TIGER WOODS**, about his mom

*"There's not a day, I don't think, when I won't think about
my Dad. Especially on the golf course. There are so many
wonderful memories, I think back on it and always smile."*
—**TIGER WOODS**, two months after the death of his father, Earl

"He made golf fun." —**NANCY LOPEZ**, on her father

*"He was always so positive, so encouraging. He was the one who made me believe I could do anything out there. He worked hard to give me all he could. I respected him so much for that. He wanted to give me a better life."*
—**NANCY LOPEZ**, on her father

"My father told me 'There will be a time and place in your career you will treasure.' I know that this was the moment he was talking about."
—**IAN WOOSNAM**, Captain of the 2006 European Ryder Cup Team on the eve of the matches (the European team won)

*"I'm very proud of my dad. He's a tremendous fighter, got an unbelievable will, and you know, hopefully he's passed a little bit of that to me."*
—**TIGER WOODS**, during his father's battle with cancer

"My father once said to me when I had a little problem with my game and wasn't doing very well, he said, 'Arnie, just remember one thing, It's a game. Play it like a game.' And I've always remembered that and I tried to do that." —**ARNOLD PALMER**

*"Family is the biggest part of my life, it's hard to miss."*
—**CHRIS DIMARCO**

"The luckiest break I ever got was Dad being transferred down to Austin." —**TOM KITE**

*"He never put any pressure on me. He'd ask 'Did you try to do your best? If you did, then don't feel bad."*
—**NANCY LOPEZ**, on her father

"When I finally did beat him the whole dam broke lose and I never looked back. He made it very clear that it wasn't because of anything he did."
—**TOM KITE**, on the first time he beat his Dad

*"The more I go through life, the smarter he seems to get."*
—**TIGER WOODS**, reminiscing on his father's advice

"You have to have a team." —**NATALIE GULBIS**

*"My Dad was my only teacher from youth to 30 years old."*
—**RAYMOND FLOYD**

"He only knew what he was going to tell you in a few amount of words but usually they were very fundamental in sound." —**BEN CRENSHAW**, on Harvey Penick

*"I think you have to analyze your performance and where you went wrong. Too many people are afraid to look deep down and look at where you made mistakes. That's not always easy to do, to be honest with yourself. That's something my father always instilled in me and even to this day, sometimes it's difficult, but you have to take an honest look and have an honest evaluation of your performance."* —**TIGER WOODS**, March 2007

"He told me, 'You got to believe in Ben.'"
—**BEN CRENSHAW**, on Harvey Penick

*"The first time I had a club in my hand, my father was teaching me and he still teaching me."* —**SAM TORRANCE**

"I've always found that those individuals have that human touch. How ever they developed it, whether it came naturally or whether hey developed it consciously, that's what attracts me and that's what really stands out for me with those players." —**PETER JACOBSEN**

*"For everything to come full circle and me to be out here and be able to win it, it's pretty cool."* —**BILL HAAS**, about his dad, Jay, being there for first win at the Bob Hope Classic

"I want to tell you a little bit about growing up in Rhode Island. It's not a likely place for a PGA Tour player, but I had some great parents. I was very lucky. My dad is here in the audience with his wife, and my mom is right there. They were golfers that kind of introduced me to the game at a young age, and they never pushed me to play but they thought that was a good place to hang out. There wasn't a lot of trouble you were going to get in if you were playing 36 holes in a day. I still believe that."
—**BRAD FAXON**, 2005 Payne Stewart Award recipient

*"Ben talks to me on every hole. When we go to the green he always says, 'You're away.'"* —**JIMMY DEMARET**, about Ben Hogan

"He always said, "Luck plays a great part in the game" and he said "I can only prepare as best as I can" He taught us in a very different way" He never taught any two players the same."

—**BEN CRENSHAW**, about Harvey Penick

*"I believe the most powerful forces in the universe are faith, love, and passion. They are the foundation upon which a happy, productive, and purposeful life is based. We all possess an infinite capacity for each. The key to fulfilling our passion is to identify it, commit to follow it, and nurture its possibilities."* —**MATTHEW E. ADAMS**

"I finally found the guy I used to know on the golf course. It was me." —**JACK NICKLAUS**, after winning the 1986 Masters

*"In post-round interviews, it is interesting how often golfers will review a particular shot they hit by stating 'we decided to play it below the hole…we dropped down one club and hit a seven iron…our game plan was to remain patient and wait for the opportunities, etc.' Of course, these golfers are referring to their caddies when speaking in a plural form. The golfer and his*

*caddie are more than just a team; they are virtually one as they face the challenges of tournament golf. Just like a touring golfer, we do not need to face life's challenges alone. Family, loved ones, and friends are all valuable sources of support. In many of the more complex areas of our lives there are countless experts available to us to help make our journey a little easier. Getting help from an expert is not a sign of weakness. On the contrary, it is the sign of someone who is open to the highest levels of learning and accomplishment."* —**MATTHEW E. ADAMS**

"Every time you swing at it, try to hit it somewhere. Don't miss it. Make contact every time."

—**DOMINGO LOPEZ**, to his young daughter,

Nancy, when teaching her the game

*"He dedicated his life to the teaching of the game and I'll always have a smile on my face for the rest of my life because they know that was in Harvey's memory and I got to play well for him. I'm very convinced that the Lord was honoring me through Harvey. It was an amazing week. I had a lot of help from a lot of different places."*

—**BEN CRENSHAW**, upon his 1995 Masters victory

only days after Harvey Penick passed away

"Hit the fairway. The rough is out of bounds."

—**NANCY LOPEZ**, on the advice her father, Domingo,

gave her when she was learning the game

*"When you take into account what's happened off the course, it's my worst year…Golf does not compare to losing a parent."* —**TIGER WOODS**, on 2006, a year in which he won two Major championship titles and a six event win streak but lost his Father Earl, in May

"For every 100 men who try out for the tour, 99 won't make it." —**TONY JACKLIN**, on the advice his father gave him to work hard

*"It's kind of cool to see these people light up when they see us."* —**CHRIS DIMARCO**

## CHAPTER 6

# A Funny Bounce

## Uncommon Concentration

Paired with Ben Hogan at the Masters, 1948 champion Claude Harmon was the second to hit his tee shot at the par 3, 12th hole. Hogan had already negotiated a shot to within ten feet of the cup. Choosing a mid-iron, Harmon struck a shot that never left the flagstick, resulting in a hole-in-one. The patrons screamed wildly as the two men strode to the green and Harmon proceeded to pick his ball from the hole. However, throughout all this, Hogan remained silent, deep in his almost trance-like state of competitive concentration. After Harmon retrieved his ball, the supportive cheers respectfully went silent for Hogan's birdie attempt, which he made. With the honor on the next tee, Harmon struck his tee shot and noticed Hogan making his way over to him, clearly intending to say something and no doubt to congratulate him for his rare feat. Instead, Hogan's words were a reflection of the singular mindset in which he insulated himself, stating that he had been *"waiting years to make a two on that hole!"*

## DEEP POCKETS AND ALLIGATOR ARMS

Sam Snead had an equal reputation for being a fervent bettor on the golf course, even if in a casual round of golf, and for being very frugal in the distribution of funds for the same purposes. In other words, if you were competing against Sam Snead, you were in for a match. Remember, Sam Snead is a man who still carried a one-iron in his bag at 89 years old!

On one such occasion, rare though it may be, ole' Sam finished on the losing side of a match, having been done in by a heavy allotment of handicap strokes to his opponent and an oft-shaky putter in his later years. At the conclusion of his round, Snead cracked open his wallet, rubbing a twenty dollar bill between his fingers in order to ensure he did not accidentally pull out more than the debt demanded. Snead handed over the Jackson like he was handing over his soul. Delighted, his amateur slayer pronounced, "I am going to have this framed!"

"Oh," replied Sam. "Give me back the twenty. I'll write you a check."

"The biggest problem has been my putting because
I've got nowhere to put my elbows. I used to be
able to put my elbows on my love handles and putt
pretty good. Now they're all over the place."

—**JOHN DALY**, after losing 100 pounds

*"Fat guys don't yip."* —**JOHNNY MILLER**

"You can play the [front] tees if you want. Otherwise, you can stand back here like a man and weep." —**TIGER WOODS**, to former President Bill Clinton

*"Half of golf is fun, the other half is putting."*
—**PETER DOBEREINER**

"I've always seen it on TV and I've always wanted people to pour beer on me." —**MICHELLE WIE**, after her first win on the LPGA at the Lorena Ochoa Invitational.

GOLFER: *"What do I owe you?"*
IRISH CADDIE: *"An apology."* —**JON DUFFY**

"I like going out on the West Coast, like going to Las Vegas; you can't wait to get there and you can't wait to leave." —**STEVE ELKINGTON**

GOLFER: *"You must be the worst caddie in the world."*
SCOTTISH CADDIE: *"No sir, we couldn't 'ave a coincidence like that."* —**HENRY LONGHURST**

"I'm going to die in a tournament on the golf course. They'll just throw me in a bunker and build it up a little bit." —**LEE TREVINO**

*"I'm not sure if I qualify or not, but they're letting me in now, so the hell with everybody else!"* —**HUBERT GREEN**, World Golf Hall of Fame press conference

"I had to learn how to play out of bunkers because I used to be in so many of them." —**KEN VENTURI**

*"Dig it out of the ground like I did."* —**BEN HOGAN**

"I'm only scared of three things: lightning, a side hill putt, and Ben Hogan." —**SAM SNEAD**

*"The first tournament I played, I remember walking through the locker room and Davis Love was walking in the opposite direction ... the guy looked 9 feet tall."* — **PAUL GOYDOS**, 2011

"When your caddie is rattling in the pocket to see if he's got a provisional ball when you're standing over the drive, you know you've got some sort of a problem." —**HENRIK STENSON**

*"Putting affects the nerves more than anything. I would actually get nauseated over a three-footer."* —**BYRON NELSON**

"I don't fear death, but I sure don't like those three-footers for par." —**CHI CHI RODRIGUEZ**

*"It's always more meaningful to do it when you absolutely have to."* —**TIGER WOODS**

"That sounds good!" —**LOUIS OOSTHUIZEN**, when introduced as the "Champion Golfer of the Year"

*"What is this old, abandoned golf course?"* —**SAM SNEAD**,
when he saw St. Andrews for the first time

"I speak three languages; my native Swedish, British English and American English." —**HENRIK STENSON**

*"If it were not for you, Walter, this dinner tonight would be downstairs in the pro shop and not in the ballroom."*
—**ARNOLD PALMER** to Walter Hagen

"My family was so poor they couldn't afford kids. The lady next door had me." —**LEE TREVINO**

*"Golf is good for the soul. You get so mad at yourself you forget to hate your enemies."* —**WILL ROGERS**

"Golf has probably kept more people sane than psychiatrists have." —**HARVEY PENICK**

*"You have one problem. You stand too close to the ball after you've hit it."* —**SAM SNEAD**

"When you go head to head against Nicklaus, he knows he's going to beat you, you know he's going to beat you, and he knows you know he's going to beat you." —**J. C. SNEAD**

*"They call it golf because all the other four letter words were taken."* —**RAYMOND FLOYD**

"Trevino has more lines than the L & N Railroad."
—**FUZZY ZOELLER**

*"Arnold didn't know which way to throw that thing when he first started playing. He'd throw it back this way, and then he would be back there picking it up. I told him, say, 'Arnold, throw it down the fairway, we'll pick it up on our way.' I'm not the only guy that's ever thrown a club."*
**—TOMMY BOLT**

"It is a lot nicer looking down on the grass instead of looking up at it." **—ARNOLD PALMER**

*"If a lot of people gripped a knife and fork the way they do a golf club, they'd starve to death."* **—SAM SNEAD**

"By the time you get to your ball, if you don't know what to do with it, try another sport." **—JULIUS BOROS**

*"It's better to be 70 years young than 40 years old."*
**—GARY PLAYER**

"They're all top heavy. They've got too much hair."
**—BEN HOGAN**, on younger golfers

*"If you take out that eight I made on 17 yesterday and I'm right back in this golf tournament."*
**—GRAEME MCDOWELL**

"Drive for show, but putt for dough." **—BOBBY LOCKE**

*"The ardent golfer would play Mount Everest if somebody would put a flagstick on top."* **—PETE DYE**

"God save that tour if he ever learns to drive the golf ball." —**LEE TREVINO**, on Tiger Woods

*"You know those two-foot downhill putts with a break? I would rather see a rattlesnake."* —**SAM SNEAD**

"I hate this game. And I can't wait till tomorrow to play it again." —**JEFF SLUMAN**

*"I made that putt, it just didn't go in."* —**TOM KITE**

"Never bet with anyone you meet on the first tee who has a deep suntan, a 1-iron in his bag, and squinty eyes." —**DAVE MARR**

*"Golf is a fascinating game. It has taken me nearly forty years to discover that I can't play it."* —**TED RAY**

"You can't go into a shop and buy a good golf game." —**SAM SNEAD**

*"Hell, I'd putt sitting up in a coffin if I thought I could hole something."* —**GARDNER DICKINSON**

"If you call God to improve the results of a shot while it is still in motion, you are using 'an outside agency' and subject to appropriate penalties under the rules of golf." —**HENRY LONGHURST**

*"I can airmail the golf ball, but sometimes I don't put the right address on it."* —**JIM DENT**

"I don't fear anything. The only thing I fear is that my wife will cremate me in a yellow sweater."
—**LEE TREVINO**

*"Miss this little putt for fifteen hundred? I should say not."*
—**WALTER HAGEN**

"I always loved what Henry Cotton did when he retired. Once he retired, he never putted another four-footer. I've putted enough of those in my life."
—**JACK NICKLAUS**

*"My dad said he never had to tell me to do my homework, never laid a hand on me and never raised his voice to me. That's because my mom did all that!"* —**TIGER WOODS**

"In my heyday, we never had five tee markers on the golf course. Come on, you go to some of these golf courses and they have five tee markers! What the hell does that mean?" —**LEE TREVINO**

*"At 75, without boasting, I could beat most 20 year olds at a fitness contest."* —**GARY PLAYER**

"Gatorade hasn't helped everyone." —**LEE TREVINO**

*"You want me to tell the chairman of the golf tournament, the President of the States, or Dirty Harry to pick up?? No, that's your job!!"* —**HUBERT GREEN** to tournament official during slow-some with Hope, Eastwood and Ford

"I'm definitely not thinking of retirement. But I'm definitely positioning myself for when that day comes."
—**ERNIE ELS**, 2011

*"I have a bridge game everyday at 4 o'clock, we play for money."*
—**LEE TREVINO**

"I putted with a pitching wedge and a 1-iron, it was very embarrassing, I broke my putter." —**BEN CRENSHAW**

*"Maybe an immediate goal is to shoot my age and every year it gets easier"* —**HALE IRWIN**

"The old trite saying of 'one shot at a time'? It was not trite to me. I lived it." —**MICKEY WRIGHT**

*"A lot of guys on Tour gripe about losing their laundry. I remember when I only had one shirt."* —**LEE TREVINO**

"What train?" —**BEN HOGAN**

*"What is it about a three-foot putt that can cause such unbridled fear? Why is it that otherwise fearless men and women of commerce, politics, or sport become paralyzed with overwhelming anxiety when faced with such peril?"*
—**MATTHEW E. ADAMS**

"When I die I want to be reincarnated as myself. I like all the things I like." —**DAVID FEHERTY**

*"It's good sportsmanship not to pick up lost balls while they are still rolling."* —**MARK TWAIN**

"When you're playing for $500 and you
have to borrow a penny to spot your ball,
now that's pressure." —**LEE TREVINO**

*"Put him three strokes behind anybody, and he believes
he's the favorite."* —**FRANK BEARD**, on Arnold Palmer

"Retire to what? I'm a golfer and a fisherman.
I've got no place to retire to." —**JULIUS BOROS**

## CHAPTER 7

# Myths and Legends

## THE UBIQUITOUS WALTER HAGEN

I magine being third on the all-time list of Majors won and yet you played the majority of your career during an era when only three of the game's four Majors even existed? Further, consider that as impressive as that fact is, Walter Hagen is revered for raising the status of golf professionals above a simple servant class and for his starring role as golf's consummate showman.

Hagen was born in 1892 into a humble, middle class family living near Rochester, New York. He was one of five children, four girls and Walter. His father, a Dutch immigrant, was a blacksmith and seemingly a world apart from the person his only son was destined to become. Walter's relationship with his working class father was a complicated one and short of a dossier on its complexities, the fact that his father never once saw him compete until the 1931 U.S. Open, two years past Walter's last Major victory—the 1929 Open Championship, speaks volumes.

Hagen was one of those rare individuals who was clearly before his time. He possessed a drive, intellect, and perhaps most importantly, a vision of the emergence of the game and his starring role in it, that ushered in the modern game as we know it.

Excelling in various sports as a youth, particularly baseball and golf, Hagen ultimately decided that golf would be his vehicle to stardom and the lifestyle that he aspired to live. Blessed with unnerving self-confidence, Hagen first came to national prominence at the 1913 U.S. Open at The Country Club in Brookline, Massachusetts. It was at this Open where a twenty-year-old amateur named Francis Ouimet beat the two top golfers in the world, Brits Harry Vardon and Ted Ray, in an eighteen hole playoff, to mark one of the greatest upsets of all time.

Finishing one stroke back was a brash twenty-one year old assistant professional from the Country Club of Rochester, named Walter Hagen. The following year, at Midlothian in Chicago, Hagan won the first of his two U.S. Open titles in a gutsy performance over a highly experienced field. Hagen stumbled to the tee box on the first day, reeling from the effects of a less-than-fresh lobster he had consumed the evening before. Coupled with the stifling heat of a Chicago summer, the young professional hits shots that were simply ugly, following them with recovery shots that were brilliant. His up and down round, reflective of the way he spent the night before, not only established a new course record and the lead in the tournament, but would also serve as a microcosm of the rest of his career.

Among his many firsts, Hagen may well have been the game's first mental coach, even if he alone was the primary beneficiary of his philosophies. Hagen was unfettered by shortcomings, mistakes or even failure. He saw those mundane consequences as the byproducts to success. Therefore he played a fearless game for his posture was that he would take the risks necessary to succeed with a perspective that if he did not win then it did not matter if he finished second or last.

Further, he anticipated adversity, even expecting it. He claimed that he expected five bad shots a round (some accounts have the number at seven), so that when a poor shot would arrive, he did not see it as a omen for his round collapsing, but rather, with almost a sense of relief that he got it out of the way and only good things lie ahead.

Perhaps this was the only mental posture one could have when your game was subject to so many wayward shots, but whatever the root, he played the game with a liberty that left him unshackled by fear and thus, able to think clearly when the pressure was consuming his competition. Augmenting his mental fortitude was his supreme ability to concentrate on the here-and-now, the shot at hand, despite carrying on a never-ending performance for the galleries was another distinctive feature of this great champion.

So consummate were his abilities to recover, persevere, concentrate and execute that in 1926 he defeated the great amateur Bobby Jones by a score of 12 and 11 during a 72-hole exhibition. Hagen displayed his game in all of its classic eccentricities through the match. Shots veered wildly, both left and right, without anyone, including Hagen, knowing what direction they were likely to go. However, each time he would hit amazing recovery shots and coupled with an extraordinary short game and putting stroke, he would leave opponents in a frustrated heap. Jones was no different, commenting after the match, "When a man misses his drive, and then misses his second shot, and then wins the hole with a birdie, it gets my goat."

Armed with such skills, Hagen was a consummate match play competitor. Competing back in the days when the PGA Championship was match play, Hagen won 22 consecutive matches. While his ability to win holes was consummate, his ability to read an opponent's psyche was equally as strong.

Hagen was a master at drawing opponents into his web, engaging them in discussions of national exhibition tours where their talents would earn them fame and fortune, causing his opponents to begin to concentrate on the spoils of victory, before the victory had been earned. Then, with equal proficiency, Hagen would flip a mental switch, giving 100% concentration to the shot at hand, and deliver a crushing blow. He was known to march up to the tee box when his opponent had the honor and confidently whip a club from his bag that was either far too much or far too little than for what the shot called. Time and again, his unsuspecting opponents would fly a green or come up woefully short, only to have Walter slip the ruse club back into his bag and proceed with the club he had always intended on using.

Hagen foresaw the celebrity power of an athlete who could work magic with a golf club and ball and took full advantage of his foresight by booking exhibitions around the world and maximizing every opportunity for publicity. Hagen enjoyed life to the fullest and he is reported to have shown up on the first tee of many an event still wearing the apparel from the night before (Hagen was an impeccable dresser and was well aware of what he was doing). He once showed up on the first tee in a top hat and tails. He was the first golfer to hire an agent and his agent only built on "The Haig's" already larger-than-life reputation.

Hagen was equally at ease with winning Majors as he was rubbing shoulders with Kings and barons of industry. As such, Hagen is rightfully credited with elevating the status of the profession by refusing to allow the star of the show, himself, to be treated with anything less than treatment befitting his status. His posture in this regard was a radical departure from the norm and was met with considerable consternation at the onset.

Once, while competing at the Open Championship at Royal St. George's, Hagen was refused admittance into the clubhouse, required instead to change in the cramped offices of the golf professional's office. Instead, Hagen hired an Austro-Daimler limousine to ferry him back and forth from his posh hotel in the city, parking the eye-catching automobile in front of the clubhouse and using it to change his cloths and eat his meals. Hagen went on to win the tournament. The following year, at the Open Championship at Royal Troon, where he finished second, he was asked to come into the clubhouse for the awards ceremony. He refused the offer, countering that if he was not invited in the clubhouse during the tournament proper, he certainly would not enter now. He said that tournament officials could make the presentation in the nearby pub where he had been spending his leisure hours. Hagen's trail blazing accomplishments on behalf of golf professionals were recognized by Arnold Palmer at a testimonial dinner for Hagen, when he stated, "If not for you, Walter, this dinner tonight would be downstairs in the pro shop, not the ballroom."

Walter Hagen was such a colorful character that it is easy to overlook his immense talent. However, he would finish his career having won the PGA Championship five times (and an amazing four in a row from 1924–1927), the Open Championship four times and the U.S. Open twice, for a total of 11 Major victories. His other international titles included the French Open, Belgian Open and the Canadian Open. He also won the Western Open, considered a Major at the time he played, five times (this is an important note because the world is willing to concede that Jones' Grand Slam included two "Majors," the U.S. Amateur and the British Amateur, while those same two events are not considered to be "Majors" today, so as a matter of equity, Hagen could be considered to have actually won 16 Majors).

Hagen did compete in the Masters, known at that time as the Augusta National Invitational, however, as the Masters did not even begin until 1934, Hagen was well past his prime. Hagen was institutional in the development of the Ryder Cup once again seeming to grasp the event's eventual magnitude, playing a pivotal role in the first event in 1927 at Worcester Country Club (won by the Americans) and playing on the first five teams and finishing with an overall record of 7-1-1. He would serve as a non-playing captain in 1937 leading the American squad to an 8 to 4 victory.

As life sometimes includes ironic, if cruel twists of fate, Hagen, a life-long smoker, would suffer from cancer of the larynx, which would rob the great communicator of the ability to speak and ultimately take his life at the age of 76 on October 5, 1969.

"I was lucky to win. I've never been happier to get any cup, and I never worked so hard nor suffered so much, either." —**BOBBY JONES**, on his 1930 British Amateur victory

*"We always made each other so much better."*
—**BEN CRENSHAW**, on Tom Kite

"Bobby Jones' incredible and improbable march to the 'Impregnable Quadrilateral' the Grand Slam, in 1930, would not have happened without Jones' ability to remain patient until luck, or, as he called it, 'Lady Fortune' turned his way. Many a lesser golfer would have folded early in the cause as fate dealt blow after blow to Jones' efforts, yet at each occurrence, Jones demonstrated an amazing capacity to harness opportunity from these situations rather than simply submit and lament his fate to forces out of his control." —**MATTHEW E. ADAMS**

*"He was the most dedicated practitioner of all time. His tenacity had no equal."* —**PAUL RUNYAN**, on Ben Hogan

"In 1954, Gene Sarazen was asked by a sporting goods company he endorsed to check out the merits of a young amateur named Arnold Palmer. Sarazen reported back that Palmer 'lunged' at the ball and he concluded, '…the kid would never amount to much.'" —**MATTHEW E. ADAMS**

*"You know, it was funny. Ben never talked. Anybody that said something he'll turn around and just stare and stare at them. He was a dealer and you could not tell whether he was mad or glad or what."* —**SAM SNEAD**, about Ben Hogan

"The only emotion Ben [Hogan] shows in defeat
is surprise. You see, he expects to win."
—**JIMMY DEMARET**

*"If you didn't take lessons from Harvey, you took lessons
from somebody who took lessons from Harvey"*
—**TOM KITE**

"They were giants in our state. To have known these
gentlemen and talked to them, I find myself very
blessed to call them my friends." —**BEN CRENSHAW**,
about Texas golfing legends

*"Francis Ouimet's triumph over Harry Vardon and Ted
Ray in the 1913 U.S. Open was front-page news. Not only
is it credited with being the impetus for the explosive and
sustained growth of golf in the United States, but the victory
by the young man who would not give up has also inspired
millions to have the courage to believe in themselves,
regardless of the field of battle, and not to allow their level
of accomplishment and success to be defined by the limited
view of others."* —**MATTHEW E. ADAMS**

"They have given me more hope, because now there
is a part of me that feels like I'm fighting for them."
—**KEN GREEN**, following his horrific accident, on the fans who
have supported his recovery

*"Everyone does well when they play well, but if you can do well in those periods where your not quite there, that's what really adds up to a really good career."* —**GEOFF OGILVY**

"You can't wait to do it, but as soon as you start doing it, you can't wait to get home."
—**LEE TREVINO**, on exercise and old age

*"I would not be the golfer I am today without all the help I have received from Ernie Els."* —**LOUIS OOSTHUIZEN**

"Everyone who lives in America has won the lottery." —**GARY PLAYER**

*"In this game you have to be selfish."* —**CHRIS DIMARCO**

"Walking the fairways Thursday through Sunday is the greatest job in the world." —**CHRIS DIMARCO**

*"Through teaching, you learn to teach better."*
—**LARRY RINKLER**

"It makes me think how lucky I've been."
—**BEN CRENSHAW**

*"I call it a bumble bee year, and bumble bees beat the odds because aeronautically they are not supposed to be able to fly."* —**JOHN MAGINESS**

"You really only have four chance's to emerge as a major champion." —**HALE IRWIN**

*"I think the greater goal for me would be to be able to take what I've captured from this game and be able to take it and pass it down to someone or a group of kids or anyone who really wants to know what I think needs to happen in the game or what they can do to improve themselves not just as players but as people. To me, that's what the game is about. People. It's about people and to improve ones self through golf, to me, is the ultimate accomplishment."* —**HALE IRWIN**

"A golfer's life doesn't get much better than this." — **SAM TORRANCE**

*"That's why the game is so great! We have great men and women and those individuals have defined the game."* —**PETER JACOBSEN**

"The ones that don't go with quality find themselves in difficulty of injury." —**GARY PLAYER**

*"I think having a faith-based life has helped me."* —**JERRY PATE**

## CHAPTER 8

# A Good Fight

## A Texas-Sized Rout

The 1967 Ryder Cup at the Champions Golf Club in Houston, Texas was, by every measure, an embarrassing rout. The American team was without the services of Jack Nicklaus, even though he had already won two U.S. Opens, three Masters, one PGA, and the one Open Championship at Muirfield, due to the strict eligibility requirements of the PGA of America. However, the team was not deficit of star power, as it was anchored by Arnold Palmer and veterans Billy Casper, Julius Boros, Gene Littler and Johnny Pott, in addition to Ryder Cup newcomers Gay Brewer, Doug Sanders, Gardner Dickinson, Al Geiberger and Bobby Nichols.

As this Ryder Cup took place before the British field was joined by the rest of Europe (which would happen in 1979), the British squad comprised seven veterans of the competition, Christy O'Connor, George Will, Neil Coles, Peter Allis, Bernard Hunt, David Thomas and Brian Huggett and rookies Malcolm Gregson, Hugh Boyle and Tony Jacklin, a man who would end up being a critical part of the swing in momentum that would see the European team begin to dominate their American counterparts in today's matches.

The American Ryder Cup team did what it was expected to do. It won. Big.

The final score of 23 ½ points to 8 ½ points served to underscore just how mismatched the Brits really were. The fifteen point spread still stands as the largest margin of victory in the history of the event. While from a British perspective it would be hard to find anything redeeming in having just lost their tenth of eleven Ryder Cups since 1947 and the end of the War, it was through this depth of despair that the British golfing authorities decided to take a hard look at every aspect of their preparation.

Loosing Captain Dai Rees, who was also the leader of the last British team to win, a decade before, recommended some dramatic changes, including adopting the larger (1.68 vs. 1.62) American golf ball for uniformity of performance against their counterparts and better ball control, softening up and using more water on their greens to make them more receptive and ultimately, faster; holding more tournaments to get the British side better prepared and even suggesting that the British golfers adopt a more "American style" of wedge and putter play that did not resemble their normal "pop" motion (which worked particularly well in an era when the speed and condition of greens could vary wildly from one course to the next on their Tour).

While in retrospect, it may be easy to wave patriotic flags, the sad reality is that this latest trouncing in a long line of American dominance nearly ended the event all together, as prominent voices were chirping that it had become such a one-sided affair that even the American television networks had turned down the chance to televise it, judging that the public would have little interest in an event in which the outcome was predetermined before the first tee shot was even hit.

Not withstanding the beating handed out by the Americans, the event was distinctive for a number of other reasons. The American squad was captained by none other than Ben Hogan. It was widely known that Ben Hogan was an intense competitor and disciplinarian, and that he had little patience (actually, none) for anyone that would dare to question his omnificent authority. One of his early decisions was to use the smaller British golf ball for this competition because it flew farther into the wind and he did not want to give up any length to the enemy. Perhaps it should not come as a surprise that an apparent, if light-hearted, challenge to Mr. Hogan would be leveled by the game's reigning king, Arnold Palmer.

A private pilot, Palmer flew his own plane to the event one day after the rest of the American squad had already arrived. While he had been given permission to arrive late, Captain Hogan seemed to greet Palmer's arrival with a seething indifference. Bursting into the large locker room at the opposite end from where Hogan was sitting, Palmer called out, "Hey, Ben, is it true we are going to use the small ball?" Hogan confirmed the fact. "Well, what if I don't have any small balls?" chided Palmer. Hogan's response was frigid, "Who said you were playing?"

Palmer played nonetheless, going 5–0, however, he did sit out the morning session on the second day. When the assembled golf media quizzed Hogan as to what possible reason he had to sit Arnold Palmer, Hogan responded with the same congeniality as he had employed with Palmer himself in their earlier locker room confrontation. When asked if he could explain Palmer's absence from the morning's pairing sheet, a glaring Hogan replied, "I could, but won't."

Perhaps the height of his Hoganesque behavior took place at the pre-match banquet. British Captain Rees was the first to introduce his team and he did so at great length, listing the individual accomplishments of each of the men in his ranks. The partisan audience applauded politely on cue. Next, Hogan strode to the podium and asked the audience to hold its applause until he was done. With that, each player on his team stood as he announced their name. He then simply said, "Ladies and Gentlemen, the finest golfers in the world." The room exploded with applause that was so great that Peter Allis would later write that at that point the British team felt, "ten down before a ball had been hit."

Hogan ruled his team with an iron fist, instituting a 10:30 p.m. curfew and barring participation in all but the official social events. He required his squad to engage in long practice sessions and in an apparent effort to motivate, was heard to utter, "I've never seen so many god-awful shots in my life," as he marched behind his team at the practice range.

Hogan's victorious captaincy would serve as his swan song with the event. To no one's shock, Hogan would finish his Ryder Cup career undefeated, both as a player ('47 and '51) and as a three-time captain in 1947, 1949 and 1967.

"I think if you look at my stats, I think my bounce back is pretty good. Any time I do have a bogey or double bogey I get straight back into it, if I recall my PGA Tour stats. I think it's pretty good in that sense. It's a mental issue, just a matter of you just get over the next one and get straight back into it, forget about it and just go on. That's the nature of the game and you've got to play golf that way."

—**STEVEN AMES**, Winner of the 2006 The Players Championship

*"I really had a good feeling about this tournament, obviously winning by 13 last week helped, but I knew I was playing well and I knew I was prepared for the tournament. But I still had to execute, I still had to perform. But having the confidence that I was playing well from my performance last week that I had prepared well from the days that I had spent here, gave me the confidence and the ease of mind, if you will, heading into the final round that I was ready. I didn't question it."*

—**PHIL MICKELSON**, 2006 Masters Champion

"If we're playing against each other, I want to beat you…That's just the way I am." —**TIGER WOODS**

*"There is not a single hole that can't be birdied if you just think. But there is not one that can't be double bogeyed if you ever stop thinking."* —**BOBBY JONES**

"Those who succeed do so because they have made a choice to be winners—to rise above the din of doubt and reject any option except to see their dreams realized by employing the power of their passion." —**MATTHEW E. ADAMS**

*"In my wildest dreams I could never imagine winning this many times and winning this many majors in my 20s. Yeah, you have wild expectations and hopefully they come true, but when you exceed your own expectations, it's very special."*
—**TIGER WOODS**

"I've got to go back to his '99, 2001 seasons and probably 2002. I mean, that five-year stretch, four-year stretch, you could have brought anybody and I think it's well documented that I said quite a few good things about him. That is just the way that he played. He played on such a level that I think Nicklaus would have had a very tough time handling him. He was probably the only guy that could have maybe played with Tiger in that stretch." —**ERNIE ELS**

*"The drive is to always get better. No matter what, you'll never get there. It's a never-ending struggle. That's the fun of it, no matter how good you play, you can always play better, which makes it exciting the next day."* —**TIGER WOODS**

"I just came here to play golf and got lucky."
—**JOHN DALY**, 1991 PGA champion

*"It doesn't matter what golf course you're on,
you still got to hit the shots."* —**RETIEF GOOSEN**

"There is no such thing as a misplaced bunker.
Regardless of where a bunker may be, it is the
business of a player to avoid it." —**DONALD ROSS**

*"Competition is even more fun than golf. I like going
down to the wire knowing somebody's going to choke,
and hoping it's not me."* —**JoANNE CARNER**

"Losers see failure as an ending. Champions see
failure as a new beginning." —**MATTHEW E. ADAMS**

*"You can talk to a fade, but a hook won't listen."*
—**LEE TREVINO**

"It's a dream come true to win at the home of golf—it's
as good as it gets. Anything could have happened but I
played really well coming in. All the hard hours I've put
in to get to this point have been a lot of fun—it's why I
made the changes to my game." —**TIGER WOODS**

*"A hungry dog hunts best."* —**LEE TREVINO**

"The pressure makes me more intent about each shot.
Pressure on the last few holes makes me play better."
—**NANCY LOPEZ**

*"Winning breeds confidence and confidence breeds winning."*
—**HUBERT GREEN**

"I kept saying to myself all day that this would be my day." —**PHIL MICKELSON**

*"I am disappointed I didn't win."* —**TIGER WOODS**

"A lot of people are afraid of winning. I was afraid I might not win." —**ARNOLD PALMER**

*"I guess all hard work and a lot of wins. Obviously I played really well. I think the key was in the second half of the year, I really putted well. Whenever I'm putting well, I have a chance of winning golf tournaments. I did well in the beginning and then it was a space in the middle where I just could not make it. My game was still pretty good and once I started making putts, confidence took over and I just was always eager to play the next tournament. I couldn't wait to get on the tee and play the next tournament."* —**VIJAY SINGH**, FedEx Cup Champion

"All I really remember about '65 is that it was so easy. When you really play well, it usually is easy. It's just, you know, I don't know, you get to the end of the week, you try to explain this, it's just driver, 9-iron; driver, wedge; driver, 8-iron, whatever it might be, and it went where I was aiming, and I looked at a putt, just knocked it in. It was one of those weeks." —**JACK NICKLAUS**, about The Masters

*"My God. I've won the Open."* —**KEN VENTURI**,
after winning the U.S. Open in 1964

"And the United States Open, it's our Open Championship. Just as you hear the Europeans talk about the British Open; that's their Open Championship. Well, this is ours. And I'm an American, and it's a proud, it was a very proud moment for me in '91, when I got to hoist that trophy. It was very special. And the feeling you get, you can't really describe it, unless you understand the competition we go through." —**PAYNE STEWART**

*"Once I knew the putt was pretty straight up there, I felt really confident I could make it. I just didn't let myself think about anything else then but making the putt."*

—**ADAM SCOTT**, on his winning putt at the 18th hole, 2004 The Players Championship

"I think if I ran for mayor there at Waterville it would be a landslide. I don't know why they have accepted me so much, but we have a very good time there. We get into the pub and we get on the piano and I bring my harmonicas out and next thing you know it is about 4 o'clock in the morning and you go home." —**PAYNE STEWART**, about Waterville, Ireland

*"I didn't so much win the second U.S. Open; I hung on and I survived while everybody else kind of went south. And that's what happens."* —**CURTIS STRANGE**

"I didn't come over here to finish second."
—**VIJAY SINGH**

*"I just love the Ryder Cup, I couldn't live without it."*
—**SERGIO GARCIA**

"One of these days they're going to be as rich as our boys and they'll be easier to beat."
—**DAN JENKINS**, on the European Advantage in the Ryder Cup

*"Greatest golfing experience I've ever had."*
—**LARRY NELSON**, on the 1981 Ryder Cup
in which he went undefeated

"This is much bigger." —**IAN WOOSNAM**, on comparison
to being named Captain of the 2006 European Ryder Cup Team
and winning the Masters in 1992

*"I was an 'international grand slam' winner and that was the biggest thrill of my life because I had to do it after 50."*
—**GARY PLAYER**

"My motto is, I'm never scared of anybody, not even Tiger Woods." —**IAN WOOSNAM**, Captain of
the 2006 European Ryder Cup Team on the eve of the matches
(the European team won)

*"My last win is a win I will always remember."*
—**JIM GALLAGHER**

"Knowing they were Texans made us try much harder."
—**BEN CRENSHAW** aspiring to play as well as Texas' golfing legends

*"I know how hard it is to dominate. I know
how hard it is to win out there."* —**LEE TREVINO**

"My 9 Majors on the Senior tour were a far greater
effort then the 9 Majors on the regular tour, because I
had to do that after the age of 50 I've won more Majors
on the senior tour than any other player in history."
—**GARY PLAYER**

*"I won first place and that was my first check."*
—**RAYMOND FLOYD**

"In the back of my mind, I said this is a great, great
chance here and I just tried to hold myself together
and it was very difficult for me to do because Augusta
is a very emotional golf course. You can play some
of the most thrilling shots there, and you can play
some very dangerous shots and I think you have to
pull them off in order to get ahead. You can't
go around Augusta playing safe the whole time,
you'll never win. You have to take some chances,
they are thrilling." —**BEN CRENSHAW** after 1995 Masters

*"I felt like wow, I beat all the big guys!"* —**SAM TORRANCE**,
on winning early in his career

"I never realized then it could mean so much."
—**SAM TORRANCE**

*"I was so nervous I could barely feel the grip."*
—**JERRY PATE**, 1976 U.S. Open Champion

"I had no feelings or emotions for beating these players. If a meteor fell out of space and hit my opponent in the head, I would go ahead and putt out and go to the next hole. I'm not sure that Jack Nicklaus isn't the same way or Arnold Palmer or Curtis Strange. Do you think Curtis felt bad about beating somebody? He loved it! That's what you're out there for." —**JERRY PATE**

*"I always feel like I'm not far off."* —**BILL HAAS**

"My shoulders and my head never dropped when I topped it in the water on 17. All I was thinking about was we could hold this to par, we can make bogey, we can make double or birdie (on the last hole) and make the play offs. So I never once thought about how awful it was that I just choked. All I thought about was keep going forward and keep digging and hopefully something good can happen and it turned out it did." —**BUBBA WATSON**, about his first victory on Tour at the 2010 Travelers Championship

## CHAPTER 9

# A Revelation of Character

## THE CHAMPION WITHIN

Adversity builds character. Isn't that what they say? Perhaps it simply reveals it.

Gregory John Norman was the ultimate golfer of his era. During the time that he burst on the scene in 1983 until the ascent to the throne of a young Tiger Woods in 1998, Norman finished ranked in the top five in each of those 15 years. He was the Number One golfer in the world, seven of those 15 years, second another three years, and third in two more.

Yet, for all his magnificence, Norman would win only two Majors, both of them Open Championships. He would be in a playoff for all four, but would come up short each time. In 1986, he led all four Majors at the end of the third round, but by Sunday evening, his only victory came in the United Kingdom.

Of all the losses that this proud Australian would suffer, however, none would match the meltdown he suffered in the 1996 Masters. That was when Norman led by a pair of strokes after the first round (when he tied the Augusta course record with 63), by four after the second round, and by a seemingly insurmountable six after the third round. Surely the fourth round would be nothing but a march to the coronation, Norman waltzing home to finally get his Masters green jacket after a career of near misses.

Except for one obstacle—a wily old veteran named Nick Faldo. The 38-year-old Faldo in 1996 was near the end of his long string of excellence—he had won 35 times internationally, three times was the Open champion, twice had won the Masters, both times in playoffs. And in 1996, he birdied the 18th hole Saturday, to get into the final pairing with Norman on Sunday. Anyone else in that situation would have been awed by Norman's huge six-shot advantage. Anyone, that is, except Faldo.

The whole world might have already conceded Norman the green jacket, but not Norman himself. "I've got a lot of work to do," he said after his round Saturday evening. "I've got 18 tough holes. And everybody's even—there is no lead. I just have to shoot a score."

Faldo conceded the obvious—he knew had no business thinking about a victory. "It's a long way back," he said. "But, you know, anything's possible." Possible, perhaps, but not probable, as no one really thought anyone else had the slightest chance.

Norman bogeyed the 1st hole to start Sunday, but no one took notice. He still had a five-shot lead, and his edge was still five as he played the par-3, 6<sup>th</sup>.

Faldo birdied that hole, and Norman's margin was reduced to four strokes. Well, it might not be an overwhelming victory, the patrons reasoned, but did anyone doubt that Norman would be the eventual champion? He was still playing reasonably well, and not even Faldo could predict that the Englishman might walk away Sunday evening the champion.

The 8<sup>th</sup> hole is a par-5, and Norman had birdied it three days in a row. However, he could merely par it on Sunday, and Faldo made birdie. Now the lead was trimmed to three, dangerously close with 10 holes still to be played. A murmur swept through the crowd—might this really be happening? For the first time all day, there was doubt as to who the eventual winner might be. Could Greg Norman, the best golfer in the world, really blow a six-shot lead in the tournament he wanted to win above all others?

The next four holes were perhaps the four most agonizing of Norman's illustrious career. Faldo had already shown that he wasn't about to go away, regardless of the size of his disadvantage. Norman might indeed win, but he was still going to have to earn it. Faldo simply had not made any mistakes the first eight holes, and Norman had begun to show some gaps.

The 9<sup>th</sup> hole was indeed crucial. Norman's drive was fine, but his approach shot arched up onto the green and spun off. "Just a miss-hit," he would later say. The ball wound up back down in the valley in front of the green, leading to a bogey. Faldo, still playing mistake-free golf, knocked his ball on the green and two-putted for another steady par. Now Norman's once-imposing lead was down to merely two with plenty of golf still ahead.

Back in the clubhouse, several players crowded around the television, scarcely believing what they were witnessing. Norman had toured the front nine in 38 strokes, which in itself isn't tantamount to a defeat. However, he now was obviously now out of sync. Faldo was playing brilliantly. Unless Norman could reverse the tide in a hole or two, he now was in danger of—could it be?—losing his seemingly insurmountable lead and possibly the unthinkable, the tournament.

The downslide continued at 10th hole, however. There Faldo once again made par, two-putting from 20 feet, while Norman's troubles compounded. Norman missed the green left, chipped to 10 feet, then two-putted for bogey. His lead was down to the thinnest of margins— one. Faldo had cut five strokes off Norman's advantage in just ten holes.

And at the 11th hole, Norman's lead would disappear completely. He three-putted from 15 feet away for a bogey and Faldo continued to play steadily, making yet another par. They walked off the hole with the score—unbelievably it seemed—tied.

It would only require one more hole for Norman's disintegration to be complete. The 12th hole was one more nightmarish blur. His tee-shot on this world-famous short par-3 hit the bank fronting the hole, then rolled backwards into the pond. He forlornly strode to the drop zone and wedged up to the green, two-putting from 12 feet for double bogey. Ole Reliable Faldo merely made another par. As the two walked to the tee on13, Faldo had accomplished the unthinkable—he now was ahead by two strokes.

How had Faldo done it? He hadn't performed any outlandish heroics, hadn't holed out from the fairway or shot any outrageous nine-hole scores. On only one hole had he made a score better than a par. Yet he stood unshakably throughout, making up the six-stroke deficit piece-by-piece, stroke-by-stroke.

Norman should have completely collapsed by then—but to his considerable credit, he did not. He retaliated with a birdie at the par-5, 13th hole, and came within an eyelash of making an eagle on 15 when his third-shot chip very nearly found the bottom of the cup. He stroked in the birdie putt, making it two out three holes that he had completed in sub-par totals.

But alas, the imperturbable Faldo didn't lose any ground during that stretch, either. He also birdied the 13th, reaching the green in two with a wonderful 2-iron after debating whether to hit a 5-wood. And he birdied the 15th hole when he chipped to two feet. Norman had finally righted himself, but it was too late.

Norman took his hat off to his opponent—figuratively at least— after the magnificent shot at 13. "He hit a great second shot, considering how many times he backed off it," Norman said. "That was the whole shooting match there."

Now playing the par-3, 16th still two shots behind, Norman needed a miracle—and he needed it fast. But instead he was again visited by disaster—his tee shot plopped into the water. "I just tried to hook a tee shot in there," he said, "and it hooked, all right." It proved to be a tombstone on Norman's funeral march.

In the end, though, Norman won over golf fans from around the world when he graciously congratulated Faldo. The two men warmly embraced on the 18th green after Faldo had completed a five-shot win, and he realized all too well the enormous difficulties that Norman had gone through.

"I just said, 'I don't know what to say, I just want to give you a hug,'" said Faldo.

Norman proceeded to the Masters' interview room, where he patiently dissected the loss for all the media present. Perhaps he was still in shock, but when he entered the room, he strode in with head held high, his sense of humor still strong. "I played like [expletive]," he said, grinning broadly. "I don't know any other way to put it."

However, Norman would have his difficult time when he got back home to Jupiter, Florida. There he would spend an evening on the beach, reliving the events, until he finally returned to his bed in the wee hours of the morning. He had lost majors by playoff, lost them because an opponent holed out on him or he himself disintegrated on the 72nd hole. But he had never, never lost one like this.

A somber Faldo said, "I hope I'm remembered for shooting 67 on the last day, and not what happened to Greg. But obviously, this will be remembered for what happened to Greg."

It was, perhaps, the most disappointing loss of Norman's stellar career. But an amazing thing happened. In the midst of his darkest hour, he endeared himself and won over a golfing public that could certainly identify with Norman's grief, his fragility, his humanity.

"I have had in excess of 7,500 letters. They are still coming in," a surprised Norman would reveal to the media at his next Tour event.

Somehow in losing, he had actually won something more. "Winning is not everything. It is how you play the game and how you accept your defeats. I think that is the most important thing," he would surmise.

Norman lost a Masters no one thought he could lose. But his composure through adversity and dignity in defeat helped define him as a champion in the most important game, the game of life.

"The words got lost, you know, somewhere between the brain and the mouth. And it was very difficult, but I fought through it. I went to a school to try and get over that, and I just would work my tail off. I would talk to my dog and he would sit there and listen, and he'd fall asleep, I finally learned how to do that, without stuttering all over myself."

—**TIGER WOODS**, on his childhood stuttering problem

*"Who is going to be second?"*

—**WALTER HAGEN**, frequently spoken before a competition

"I think you're not as tough and cocky as when you're young and full of energy. I got humbled. I had to reorganize my life. I had to put my faith first, my family second and my golf third." —**JERRY PATE**, 1976 U.S. Open Champion on winning golf tournaments on the Champions Tour

*"People thought I was boring. I used to just hit it in the fairway, onto the green, then hole the putt."*
—**BYRON NELSON**

"This is like winning a major off the golf course, to win this award. It's something you're not doing with your golf clubs alone. It's the way you carry yourself, the way that the guys that have won this award before have kept the traditions of the game going. But if you're an individual on the Tour and you know about this award, I think this is something that you should strive to win. When I first heard about the Payne Stewart Award, I thought in the back of my mind that would be a great thing to win some day. But I would urge now all the young players that this is an award that's as important as trying to win a major. You don't think about it maybe as a kid growing up that you want to win the Payne Stewart Award. But after you've been out here and you see what the PGA Tour is all about, you've reached a billion dollars in charitable giving, we're on our way to $2 billion as you heard. This is my finest hour, this is unbelievable. I can't say how thankful I am and how humbled this award makes me and I hope that every young guy on the PGA Tour tries to win the Payne Stewart Award. We'll be better off."

—**BRAD FAXON**, 2005 Payne Stewart Award recipient

*"I don't play in the past. I play in the present."*
**—RAYMOND FLOYD**

"I've been friends with Vijay since 1992, I think. To me, he has not changed at all. He's always been the same. He's very driven, like a lot of us out here. But definitely off the golf course, he's a very nice man. We've had our battles on the course and so forth, but, you know, he's a gentleman and he's a good friend. He's probably as relaxed as they get." **—ERNIE ELS**

*"…you cannot become a champion without the ability to cope with your emotions. That is the most important factor in becoming a winner."* **—MICKEY WRIGHT**

"I think I learn something everyday from a lot of people. You are right, I have been around and I have achieved a lot. I have a lot of experience, but I am far away from being a complete golfer. That is what keeps me excited and excited about my game that I always have something to look forward to and something to get better at." **—ANNIKA SORENSTAM**

*"The self-belief and patience over the last 10 years have really paid dividends, but it's been quite a journey. Back in '98 I was going to throw the game away and sell golf balls. I remember throwing my golf bag across a hotel room and thinking to myself 'It's all over.'"* **—MICHAEL CAMPBELL**

"It was a great joy to improve." —**BEN HOGAN**

*"I can only tell you one thing I do know for sure, I am a dreamer. There are not many people that will recognize or want to recognize that fact that they are dreamers in their own life. I continue to get up in the morning, enthusiastically, and go pick up a golf club with a thought that I can somewhere find that secret to making the cut. That's just an example, but it applies to other things in life, too, and that's why I live and the way I think and the way I feel."* —**ARNOLD PALMER**

"Good golfers learn to convert anger into productivity." —**TOMMY BOLT**

*"I love to play and to win."* —**TIGER WOODS**

"I look into their eyes, shake their hand, pat their back, and wish them luck, but I am thinking, 'I'm going to bury you.'" —**SEVE BALLESTEROS**

*"I like to set high goals, I like to motivate myself, and, I mean, first if you can believe it in your mind, I think you can do it"* —**ANNIKA SORENSTAM**

"I was at the dinner last night, and all Hall-of-Famers that are here for the induction tonight were recognized last night, and I was just, like, 'What am I doing here?' I still don't really feel like I should be among these great players. I think that will always take a long time to sink in for me. But obviously I'm still enjoying and soaking up every minute of this occasion." —**KARRIE WEBB**

*"I think I'm a pretty easy-going guy. I'm very serious when I play golf, but then everybody is. You're very serious when you're doing your job. I take my job very seriously. Outside my job, I'm a little bit easy-going."* —**VIJAY SINGH**

"I have a good attitude on the golf course. I don't have to prove a lot more, but I'm out there because I want to, because I enjoy it and I want to just play well. It's like hey, what the hell, go for it."
—**NICK FALDO**

*"They might be able to beat me, but they can't out practice me."*
—**JERRY BARBER**

"I'll never be a ceremonious golfer."
—**RAYMOND FLOYD**

*"What I've tried to maintain is just being myself and not be anything anyone else wants me to be, I've just tried to be myself, and that's probably my best advice that I can give the young players."* —**KARRIE WEBB**

"I don't ever feel like I've achieved everything in the game that I can achieve." —**HALE IRWIN**

*"Sometimes being different is a good thing."*
—JOHN DALY

"If you create a brand within yourself;
once you decide what you want to be, never let
yourself slip below that." —GREG NORMAN

*"I felt for the first time I belonged."*
—LEE TREVINO, on his success in 1971

"Of all the things that had happened today,
I thought 'At least I still have a chance,' I turned
it into a positive." —TIGER WOODS

*"I never looked as myself as a teacher. I'm teaching my
children hopefully to be good human beings but everything
else, I don't consider myself a teacher. I just try to treat
everybody well and honor God with all of the gifts that
He's given me and that's really all what I'm trying to do."*
—BERNHARD LANGER

"I think anytime you don't set yourself high
goals, you're not going to succeed very well. I
think I've got to a point where I can set them
as high as I really want, and I'd rather be a little
bit disappointed rather than being satisfied with
something like just finishing Top 10 every week."
—LUKE DONALD

*"You would think winning a Major would mellow you. It's done the opposite to me. It's made me even more obsessive. There's a huge incentive to push on. I don't think I have that attitude of some guys who are trying to prove they deserved to win it. But I certainly have the attitude that I really want to win another."*
**—PADRAIG HARRINGTON**

"I'm a good golfer and I understand golf. So far I can beat all my architects very easily in golf, so that's always nice." **—DONALD TRUMP**

*"We learned to play golf a different way, especially down here in Texas. The wind blows extremely hard, we are kind of a 'hold on generation.' We held onto the club a little longer, we held the back on the left hand toward the target a little longer. We got our speed from body movement. We were stuck in other words. We could only hit the ball a certain distance. You never found guys that came from Texas that were extremely long hitters. Most long hitters came from California or up East."* **—LEE TREVINO**

"I've gotten to know people very well through golf. I know them better in terms of personality through golf then I would ever get to know them over lunch. You see if people cheat or move the ball in the rough when no ones looking. Golf is really a good life lesson." **—DONALD TRUMP**

*"Watching somebody else miss at the title, you almost feel as bad for them as you do happy for yourself that you accomplished it."* —**CRAIG STADLER**

"The longer you play, the more you realize that a balance is healthy and it makes when you play more enjoyable and probably makes your golf game better."
—**GEOFF OGILVY**

*"I didn't come into the PGA Tour with huge expectations."*
—**STEVE STRICKER**

"I felt like maybe I can do this." —**LARRY RINKER**

*"I think the way I play the game; it lends itself to design work. I'm a strategist. I have to manage my game; I play the angles, work balls into fairways."* —**JUSTIN LEONARD**

"I was the luckiest person in the world."
—**LEE TREVINO**

*"I've never worried about what everybody thought about validating my career. I know I tried hard every day that I played."* —**TONY JACKLIN**

"I like the Cinderella stories. I like the stories of the kind of weak rising up to beat the strong."
—**TOM KITE**

*"By 1969 I accomplished my goals."* —**RAYMOND FLOYD**

"I'm not negative when I say things that aren't positive, I'm just such a perfectionist, I want to see things right and I want to see things done well. I want to see honesty among people; I want to see people do things that are great." —**JERRY PATE**

*"I think my passion and patience makes me a good teacher."* —**LARRY RINKER**

"I'm very, very fortunate. I've been luckier then most. I've been very proud of the things I've been able to achieve." —**BEN CRENSHAW**

*"I don't want to be something short of what I think I'm capable of achieving. I think you can cheat yourself when you do that regardless of what it is, and that's what has always driven me."* —**DAVIS LOVE III**

"I'm so proud to be involved in an organization such as the PGA because the common denominator on the Tour is charity." —**PETER JACOBSEN**

*"There was a flaw in my personality. I was so competitive that I couldn't see the forest for the trees. I just wanted to be the best at any cost. You see I didn't look at the guys I played with as people; I just wanted to beat them. I'd beat them and I'd giggle while I beat them. There was no humility to it. It didn't matter who they were, I wanted to say 'Line them up' that's the way it was."* —**JERRY PATE**

## CHAPTER 10

# Twist of Fate:
## Golf and Life

### THE YEAR THAT ALMOST WAS

While watching the waning moments of the 2009 PGA Championship, I started to contemplate the 2009 Major season, ready to declare the Major championships of 2009 as the greatest the sport has ever known!

It all started back in April. Against the backdrop of a global economic malaise, the Masters provided us with an opportunity to escape the unrelenting current of bad news and get lost in the beauty and serenity that can only be found in early April at Augusta National. The tournament could not have turned out to be more of a fairy tale ride. Here we had 48 year-old Kenny Perry, still fresh off his home state starring role in the triumphant efforts of the 2008 United States Ryder Cup team at Valhalla, boldly and confidently striding to victory down the stretch at Augusta.

Then we had a U.S. Open that played out like it was directly from central casting, as "the People's" Phil Mickelson, raw and untested, due to the care he was providing to his beloved wife Amy, somehow found it within himself to give the New York faithful the very thing they most craved. A coveted victory for the man they had adopted as one of their own, and a fitting revenge for a victory denied three-years earlier at the Black Course's blue-blood cousin, Winged Foot, nestled down the road in the affluent Westchester suburbs outside The City.

Then there was 2009's defining moment. At the Open Championship at Turnberry, Tom Watson literally turned back the clock, reminding us all that "59 is the new 29," matching Harry Vardon for the most Open Championships of all time.

So there I was, watching Tiger Woods lord over the field at Hazeltine, my mind drifting to the Major tournament events that would forever be remembered, each defined as a "I-remember-where-I-was-when" moment.

But…wait a minute…maybe my recall has simply become lost in misty delusional recollections as clouded (and unsettled) as the foam atop my Guinness??

Kenny Perry did indeed author a 2009 Masters performance to remember. Through three rounds the veteran played inspired golf, sharing the lead with Angel Cabrera at 11 under par. The final round began with a flash, as both Tiger Woods and Phil Mickelson would make a Sunday charge up the leader board. Mickelson birdied six holes on the front nine to score a 30, tying a tournament record. Mickelson would finish the day with a 67 and a total score of 9 under par, good for 5th place. Woods would post a final round 68, for an 8 under par total and a share of 6th place.

But it was Kenny Perry who seemed to be assured of victory, leading by two strokes with two holes to go. But, bogeys on the 17th and 18th holes would send Perry into a sudden death playoff against Chad Campbell and Angel Cabrera. Campbell would drop out after the first playoff hole, and after Perry failed to get up and down from left of the green on the second playoff hole, it left Angel Cabrera with a comfortable two putts from 15 feet to secure his first Masters victory and his second Major title.

In June, the U.S. Open returned to Bethpage's Black Course, with great anticipation. The people of New York themselves were as much a part of the story as was this storied municipal golf course that was hosting the U.S. Open for a second time. However, it was Mother Nature that decided to assert herself as one of the wettest spring and summers of all time in the northeast brought copious amounts of rain over Father's Day weekend to Long Island.

The week's drama began with Mickelson sharing that his wife Amy, battling breast cancer, had asked him to bring back the U.S. Open trophy for her hospital room. Mickelson's efforts that week were nothing short of heroic. Undone, though, by missing two par putts over the last four holes, he finished in second place a record 5th time.

Coming in ranked as the 882nd player in the world, in the final round, David Duval thrilled the crowd with three straight birdies on the back nine to tie for the lead, but when a five foot par putt on the second-to-last hole spun 180 degrees out of the cup it took with it, his chances for victory.

Ricky Barnes may have been a long shot, but he put up a gallant fight through three rounds. However, a front nine 40 led to a score of 76 and Barnes would settle for a share of 2nd place with Mickelson and Duval.

So it would be a two stroke victory for Lucas Glover at the 2009 U.S. Open, his win underscored by the fact that he won the National Championship as only the second player in 25 years to win a Major in which he had never previously made the cut (Lee Janzen was the other, in 1993), and he was the first qualifier to win the U.S. Open since Michael Campbell in 2005. This U.S. Open win also represented his 2nd career win.

July brought with it great enthusiasm as the return of the Open Championship to Turnberry's Ailsa Course was expected to be an affair when the young lions starring on golf's global stage would battle it out on the fabled links. Only the stage was commandeered by anything but a young lion, as Tom Watson seemed to channel the likes of "Old Tom," as in Old Tom Morris, the Scottish legend. Golf can be a magical experience and the show put on by Tom Watson was one putt short of being the most significant event in the long history of the game.

I was privileged to witness the events at Turnberry, joining the legions who watched Watson's magical march evolve from the impossible, to the improbable, to the possible, to the likely, and finally, ultimately, to *what could have been.*

The 18th green at Turnberry's Ailsa Course was lined on each side with massive grand stands, only, unlike those which we've grown accustomed to week in and week out, these grand stands were not reserved for VIPs or corporate big-wigs. The price of admission into these coveted seats was to stand in line and wait for a seat to open up, and so I did with my friends. Soon, we scored four perfect seats near the top of the grand stand with a perfect view of the entire 18th Hole and great views over the rolling dune-scape that was Turnberry.

The entire property seemed bathed in a golden glow and watching huge armies of galleries migrate from one dune peak to valley made me feel very much like I was watching medieval opposing forces, the only thing missing were the army flags. If our tiny Radio Open Golf radios did not provide us with the details, then surely we could feel the flow and ebb of the day simply by listening to the battle cries of joy and moans of agony rising up from different parts of the golf course as the situation mandated. No doubt, those of us on the 18th hole made our fair share of joyous and distressed wails as well.

Tom Watson's drive on the 18th hole in regulation was brilliant. Leading by one, facing a relatively simple second shot, there did not seem to be anything that could keep him from being crowned as the man who would own the greatest golf story of all time. Then, fate and circumstance intervened.

Watson hit a perfect second shot into the 18th green. Many will tell you he hit it too far, but they were not there. Rather, he hit it just too short, his ball landing on a small knoll in the green that was imperceptible on a television screen, cruelly catapulting his ball forward without the benefit of spin and landing in an untenable position, where once more, the television screen images tended to diminish the severity of the task left before him. The viewing world may have held its breath over Old Tom's last putt, but there was a discernable resignation among many eyewitnesses, merely seeing where the unfortunate approach shot had come to rest. It was as if fate had already chosen its victor and the final torturous events that had yet to fully play themselves out were merely a formality.

The rest, as they say, is history and accounts that the galleries were not gracious to Stewart Cink after his playoff dominance of Watson, are false. While virtually everyone there was sad about Old Tom's demise, Cink was greeted with congratulatory respect befitting the Champion Golfer of the Year.

Then there was the final chapter in the year of *almost* Hollywood finishes in the Majors, the 2009 PGA Championship. Here was David slaying Goliath. For the very first time in a Major, Tiger Woods would fail to close the deal while leading after three rounds. Instead, it was Y.E. Yang who became the third golfer of 2009 to win his fist Major. It would be most understated to declare Yang's victory as an upset.

And so, there I was, clarity setting in as the lights faded over Hazeltine, realizing that golf is not a game defined by the sentimentality of those standing along the rope lines or perched in the grandstands, or watching (or listening) at home. The game of golf, like the game of life awards its spoils not to those who we simply *want* to win, those who we feel *should* win, or "*deserve*" to win. No, golf's victories go to those who earn it over the course of an entire tournament, until the very last putt drops into the cup.

If any of us had set out to write the perfect script for the 2009 Majors, then the game gave us tantalizing glimpses into what those story lines *could* have been. But in the end, the game did what the game does, as the winners were deemed by merit, not sentiment. Not withstanding the pulling of our heartstrings, that is exactly the way it should be.

"As you walk down the fairway of life you must smell the roses, for you only get to play one round."
—**BEN HOGAN**

*"You have to play the rules of golf just as you have to live by the rules of life. There's no other way."* —**BABE DIDRIKSON**

"A bad attitude is worse than a bad swing."
—**PAYNE STEWART**

*"When you lose your temper after missing a shot, the chances are you will miss the next shot, too."*
—**JULIUS BOROS**

"I believe if society in general conducted itself the way we golfers do, this would be a much better world." —**RAY FLOYD**

*"If we are all destined to miss our share of the three-foot putts of life, then we can at least seek to increase our odds of success through preparation, and a conviction that not only are we capable of success, but we deserve it."*
—**MATTHEW E. ADAMS**

"Thinking instead of acting is
the number-one golf disease." —SAM SNEAD

*"I had a fifteenth club in my bag this week. It was
Harvey Penick."* —BEN CRENSHAW, after 1995 Masters

"If the mind is full of fear or failure; a dread of the
next approach, a persistent thought of three putts
although the green is still far away, then, in my
experience, there is but one thing that can at all
help and that is to see the humor of the situation."
—JOYCE WETHERED

*"Success is measured certainly in different levels in
different ways. If you play as well as you can and really
don't make mistakes and get beat, you have a successful
week. And if you base it solely on position or outcome of
the golf tournament, I don't know if you could ever have
any satisfaction. You know, there's very few players who
have ever played this game, I daresay, that if they played
their best, still couldn't be beat by other people. I mean,
you know, you could probably name a couple. Most
people agree, if they play their best, most other people
would not beat them. So if you're measuring it just solely
on winning golf tournaments, I think you're looking
at it the wrong way."* —DAVID DUVAL

"The guy who believes in happy endings is going to play consistently better golf than the man who approaches every act of existence with fear and foreboding." —**TONY LEMA**

*"How do you envision yourself when you fantasize a round of golf in your mind? What is the flight of your golf ball? Is it a weak slice, or is it a powerful, long, soaring drive? How do you envision yourself in your inner mind's eye in other stressful situations? How do you see yourself when you want to ask your boss for a raise or ask a difficult customer to place a large order? Are these situations so discomforting that you do not even want to consider them in your visualization, when you can easily craft the image however you choose? Do you allow yourself to be a champion or to slink away in defeat? Your dreams are more than wishful thinking, they define your ambition."* —**MATTHEW E. ADAMS**

"A buoyant, positive approach to the game is as basic as a sound swing." —**TONY LEMA**

*"In golf, as in life, you get out of it what you put into it."*
—**SAM SNEAD**

"The most rewarding things you do in life are often the ones that look like they can't be done."
—**ARNOLD PALMER**

*"When it comes to the game of life, I figured I've played the whole course."* —**LEE TREVINO**

"Golf reflects the cycle of life. No matter what you shoot, the next day you have to go back to the first tee and begin all over again and make yourself into something." —**PETER JACOBSON**

*"Success depends almost entirely on how effectively you learn to manage the game's two ultimate adversaries, the course and yourself."* —**JACK NICKLAUS**

"Golf is a lot like life. When you make a decision, stick with it." —**BYRON NELSON**

*"In our quest to master a game that cannot be mastered, golf is foremost about self-discovery. A person is revealed to the world in a round of golf. Even more so, we are revealed to ourselves. Our character, integrity, and morality are all put to the test, and our ability to handle pressure is put to the fire. Sometimes we succeed, sometimes we fail, and if we are observant, each time we learn something new, something to keep us coming back."*
—**MATTHEW E. ADAMS**

"Love and putting are mysteries for the philosopher to solve. Both subjects are beyond golfers."
—**TOMMY ARMOUR**

*"The main idea in golf as in life, I suppose is to learn to accept what cannot be altered and to keep doing one's own reasoned and resolute best whether the prospect be bleak or rosey."*
**—BOBBY JONES**

"I've been fortunate enough to resurrect my game and get it moving in the direction I want it to go in, and that's no different then life in general that you have peaks and valleys and struggles and great times."
**—STEVE STRICKER**

## CHAPTER 11

# Royal and Ancient

## BAN GOLF!

It will come as no great surprise that the Scots and the English have had a long and sometimes contentious relationship. What may come as a bit of a surprise is how this complicated union had a significant impact on the development of the game of golf.

Feeling the need to constantly train his forces, particularly in archery, it was, so to speak, a burr in the saddle of Scottish King James II that his able-bodied men would choose to invest their time in less purposeful pursuits like, golf. So, in 1457, he banned the playing of game, along with football (soccer), opting to force his subjects to engage in activities that would hopefully result in the protection of his kingdom, rather than wasting time with something as trivial as golf.

Perhaps the King's time would have been better spent on the golf course, as the golf gods apparently got the last word. As an ardent supporter of the mechanized arms of the day, the King bolstered his forces with massive and powerful cannons to be used to reduce the castle walls of his enemies to rubble. The golf-ban-making King met his demise soon after his golf ban, as he made the mistake of stationing himself too close to one of his cannons during yet another battle against the enemies of the Crown. The art of loading a cannon with gunpowder, lighting it, and using its explosive power to blast a projectile in the direction of your enemies is a gamey proposition to say the least. Well, for King James II, this reality hit home, quite literally. You see, the cannon misfired, blowing itself to bits along with King James II.

Nonetheless, King James' successors apparently saw the wisdom of his golf ban (not withstanding the risk of earning the wrath of the golf gods) as it continued to be reiterated and upheld by both his son and grandson (although it is widely believed that the Kings still secretly played), until such time as its practicality could not stand in the way of the game that is very much a part of the Scottish identity. In 1502, King James IV signed the Treaty of Glasgow, intended to ensure ever-lasting peace with England (which, ultimately, it didn't). He also clearly possessed a practical romanticism, as he married Margaret Tudor, daughter of Henry VI, the man who signed the Treaty on England's behalf. Apparently secure in the fact that a lasting peace had been achieved, it is interesting to note that it was King James IV himself who was one of the first to take to the links, on March 29, 1506, in a match against the Earl of Bothwell, perhaps contributing to the game's

Scottish lineage as a "Royal" game. Their match took place on royal hunting grounds that are now home to the Sterling Golf Club. No record was kept for who won the match, but my money is on the King.

Perhaps most interesting of all is the fact that the Scottish ban on golf has never officially been lifted.

## THE FIRST GOLF WIDOW

Over the years, much has been said about the lament of the lonely wife who waits at home while her golf obsessed husband feeds his golfing addiction. The moniker (often self-applied), to this source of festering resentment is a "golf widow."

However, history shows us that the first "golf widow" was not left behind, rather, she was the Queen of the house, literally.

Mary Queen of Scots was born in 1542, the child of King James V and Mary of Guise. Merely a week after her birth, Mary's father died, making her an infant Queen. Mary was sent away to France to be formally educated while her mother served as regent.

Mary Queen of Scots possessed an impressive lineage. Through her grandmother, Margaret Tudor, sister to King Henry VIII, she also had a claim to the English Crown, and through her mother, ties with one of France's most powerful families, The House of Guise.

While in France, Mary played and fell in love with the game of golf. It is speculated that it was this very bond that ultimately led to her tragic demise.

At the age of 15, Mary, who was raised as a Catholic, married Francis II, son of Henri II of France and Catherine Medici of the powerful

Medici family of Italy. However, the union was over two years later with the death of Francis, resulting in Mary losing any claim to the French Crown. So, in 1560 (after the death of her mother), Mary returned to Scotland to claim her rightful position.

Mary brought her love of the game back to Scotland as well. Reported to suffer from a recurrent slice, the six-foot-tall Mary often traveled with a huge party of attendants while on the links. Due to her French rearing, most of her closest attendants were called by the French word, "cadet." It is speculated that the native Scots had difficulty pronouncing this word and, thus, the word "caddie" was introduced into the game of golf for the first time.

Mary's second husband, Lord Darnley, was murdered. Within days of her husband's sad demise, there was Mary, out slicing the ball around the links. This caused an uproar of impropriety at her failure to properly mourn her husband's death and fueling speculation that she had conspired with James Hepburn the 4th Earl of Bothwell to remove her husband and some sticky claims of accession to the throne. Mary did not help her cause when she married James Hepburn within months of the murder.

Matters grew from bad to worse as her third marriage (to the Earl) put her in conflict with other Scottish nobles whose support she desperately needed. Ultimately, the political firestorm was too much and she abdicated the Thrown to her son, James VI of Scotland (later he became James I of England). She fled to England seeking asylum.

Mary's cousin, Queen Elizabeth, was not ready to trigger a war over her arrival and Mary was put under house arrest for the next 18 years.

Mary would eventually be accused of engaging in treasonous activities and sentenced to death by the axe.

Apparently, her axe-man suffered from the same inefficient slice as Mary, as it took him three attempts to slice off her head.

"Sure, I believe in ghosts. I know there are ghosts at St Andrews. When you walk across the Swilcan Bridge you can almost see them, they're so close. The Morrises, the Auchterlonies, I'm certain they're all flying around out there." —**LEE TREVINO**

*"St Andrews, the city, and the Old Course in particular, are so much more than merely a golfing destination. For a golfer, St Andrews is quite simply a Mecca. It is a pilgrimage that anyone who truly claims to love the game must make at least once in a lifetime."* —**MATTHEW E. ADAMS**

"There's much more quality and depth today." —**RAYMOND FLOYD**

*"Back in the day when I started playing, my first PGA event was the Bing Crosby, I remember it was just about players and caddies, and gallery ropes and stakes and a concession stand and maybe an out house at the turn. There were a lot of fans but not a lot of bleachers. No sky seats, not a lot of televised golf."* —**PETER JACOBSEN**

"Laddie, a blind hole is blind only once to a man with a memory." —**TOMMY ARMOUR**

*"Of all the hazards, fear is the worst."* —**SAM SNEAD**

"If your talents are mental, you are not at a disadvantage against the physically talented person. You can plan and prepare better than he can, you can outthink him during the contest, and you can manage your game better." —**GARY PLAYER**, from *The Golfer's Guide to the Meaning of Life*

*"Reverse every natural instinct and do the opposite of what you are inclined to do, and you will probably come very close to having a perfect golf swing."* —**BEN HOGAN**

"The real success in golf lies in turning three shots into two." —**BOBBY LOCKE**

*"I'm really amazed and proud of where the game has come from and where it is today."* —**PETER JACOBSEN**

"Golfers find it a very trying matter to turn at the waist, more particularly if they have a lot of waist to turn."
—**HARRY VARDON**

*"You are meant to play the ball as it lies, a fact that may help to touch on your own objective approach to life."*
—**GRANTLAND RICE**

"At the end of the day, most of the times you make the putts with your head, not with your hands."
—**SERGIO GARCIA**

*"More matches are lost through carelessness at the beginning than any other cause."* —**HARRY VARDON**

"Play every shot so that the next one will be the easiest that you can give yourself." —**BILLY CASPER**

*"The essence of good form is simplicity."* —**BOBBY JONES**

"Aside from a battlefield or other locale of intense human drama, there is perhaps no more haunted a place in the world than St Andrews. The aura of what has gone before you embraces you as soon as you enter the ancient city. From the massive cathedral ruins to the rubble of the St Andrews castle, each element of the city seems to be a building block of anticipation to your first steps on to the historic course. It is almost overwhelming, and well worth it for a first-time pilgrim to walk the course the evening before a round, if only to confirm that your feet really do touch the earth."
—**MATTHEW E. ADAMS**

*"Never practice without a thought in mind."*
—**NANCY LOPEZ**

## THE TEST OF TIME

Imagine, for a moment, that Father Time has a face.

The image is a stolid one, unaffected by joy or grief, pleasure or pain. From his face, lined by experience, flows a beard grayed with wisdom, dignity, respect, joy and sorrow.

Pan down his body and there, at his side, flows a chain that connects, inevitably, to a watch.

Now take this legendary keeper of the years and place him in St. Andrews, Scotland. That face you see belongs to Old Tom Morris, legendary keeper of the green.

No sport venerates its past more profoundly than the royal and ancient game, and Tom Morris, Sr. is chief among its iconic characters.

Morris' life has only been transcended by his death, where, a century after his passing, time has transformed "The Grand Old Man of Golf" into a mythical figure whose image invokes the very spirit of the game.

Old Tom, as he is fondly known, spans the gap from Allan Robertson, golf's first professional, and Willie Park, Sr., its first Open champion, to The Great Triumvirate of Harry Vardon, James Braid and J.H. Taylor— and today remains in the very fiber of the game, somehow untouched by the passing of the world.

Morris, despite being age 39 when he helped found The Open, played in every tournament beginning with the inaugural one in 1860 up through 1896 when he was 75.

Morris won the British Open four times—in 1861, 1862, 1864

and 1867—the last of which came at age 46 years, 99 days—a record that remains unchallenged today.

His 1862 victory also has weathered the ages. That 13-stroke victory remains the benchmark of domination in golf's oldest championship.

Morris got his start at St. Andrews when Robertson hired him as an apprentice to work in his shop, thus changing Morris' plans of becoming a carpenter. It was there, while working in St. Andrews for Robertson, that Morris honed his abilities as a club maker, feather-ball maker and, of course, as a player.

Morris' working relationship with Robertson began to deteriorate when Morris took up using the new gutta percha ball—an invention Robertson frowned upon because it was in direct competition with his livelihood of making featheries.

Their falling out eventually saw Morris accept an invitation from Col. James Fairlie (whom Morris would later name a son after) to become the keeper of the green at Prestwick in 1851. Prestwick, the birthplace of The Open, would play host to the first 12 events and see Morris win three of the first five tournaments.

Morris returned to St. Andrews as both professional and keeper of the green in 1864—a position he held until his death in 1908. Morris was unquestionably St. Andrews' foremost resident, setting up a shop adjacent to The Old Course's 18th green, where he made clubs, appeared at tournaments and, as St. Andrews entrenched itself as golf's home, became its patriarchal figure.

Golf truly ran in Morris' blood. He fathered three sons, two of whom were successful golfers—James Fairlie, Morris, and Tommy

Morris (better known as Young Tom). Young Tom competed in his first professional event when he was only 13, winning an exhibition match in Perth and claiming the £15 first prize.

Young Tom's proficiency with a set of golf clubs is why it can be said no man not named Morris ever won an Open championship by double digits. Young Tom won four successive Opens and furthered the family's golfing prowess as the best of the day.

His first Open title came in 1868 and made him the youngest winner at age 17. He also made the first ace in British Open history that year. In 1869 and 1870 he won by 11 and 12 strokes, respectively. The latter of those margins included a round of 47, which is considered the first great round of golf. Remember in those days tournaments consisted of three rounds of 12 holes, so by way of comparison today, and in order to put this considerable achievement into perspective, think for a moment about a golfer distancing himself from the field by 12 strokes after two rounds.

Young Tom followed that round of 47 with a pair of 51s giving him a 149 total and breaking the tournament record by five shots. His 149 would stand through the remainder of the 36-hole days of The Open (1892) and, perhaps even more astounding, would the 36-hole record through 1908—well into the rubber-ball era.

In the book, *Golf's Greatest*, it was written that Young Tom "was simply too good for the available competition."

By winning the British Open in three successive years (1868-1870) Morris permanently won the Challenge Belt, the tournament's first prize, as the rules of the competition stated anyone who won three years in succession won the belt outright.

His excellence in the tournament necessitated the creation of the most recognizable trophy in golf—the Claret Jug—which he also became the first to win when the tournament returned in 1872.

What Young Tom enjoyed in quality, he, sadly, lacked in quantity. While it is true Young Tom completely altered his contemporaries' belief of how well the game could be played—he was a powerful ball striker, master of the recovery from poor lies, revolutionary with his iron play and robotically consistent with his putting—his time in the game was tragically short.

In September of 1875 Young Tom's wife passed away during child birth while delivering a still-born baby. Three months later, on Christmas Day, Young Tom himself died at age 24—often reported as dying from a broken heart but correctly credited as succumbing to a lung hemorrhage.

Indeed Old Tom had to endure the death of a grandson, daughter-in-law and son in three months' time. He would eventually have to bear the death of all three of his sons, a fate he handled with similar dignity and class as he did playing golf.

Old Tom was characterized by one of the day's most notable writers, John L. Low, as "always cheerful during a life which met with almost continual disappointments and sorrows." No one less than Horace Hutchinson said that Old Tom was a beacon of humbleness.

In Hutchinson's *The Book of Golf and Golfers* he wrote that Morris "has been written of as often as a Prime Minister, he has been photographed as often as professional beauty, and yet he remains, through all the advertisement, exactly the same, simple and kindly."

Old Tom's contributions as an architect remain as vivid as his presence in the game. During his life it is estimated he laid out or helped sculpt between 60-75 courses, including Carnoustie, Prestwick, Westward Ho!, Royal Dornoch, St. Andrews and Lahinch. His impact in this field influenced many of the most prominent designers known today, including C.B. Macdonald, Alister MacKenzie, A.W. Tillinghast, Harry Colt and Donald Ross.

Old Tom passed away at age 87 in 1908 and those turning out to pay their respects lined the entire length of South Street in St. Andrews and caused Andrew Kirkaldy to remark, "There were many wet eyes among us for Old Tom was beloved by everybody."

In 1983 the Golf Course Superintendents Association of America began presenting the Old Tom Morris award, which is awarded to an individual who, through a continuing lifetime commitment to the game of golf, has helped to mold the welfare of the game in a manner and style exemplified by Old Tom Morris.

Proving Old Tom's place in the game remains indelible, the Royal Bank of Scotland issued a special £5 note in 2004 commemorating the 250th anniversary of The Royal and Ancient Golf Club of St. Andrews. The note featured the likeness of Old Tom Morris.

Perhaps Old Tom's place in the game is best memorialized by the most famous finishing hole in golf—the 18th hole at The Old Course in St. Andrews. For it is this hole that was named in his honor.

Like the game whose image he reflects, Old Tom has certainly stood the test of time.

## CHAPTER 12

# To Believe

## THE OVERBITE

Tiger Woods' reputation for tackling a tournament with overwhelming performances is well known. His Major victories at the 1997 Masters (breaking records by winning by 12 strokes, setting a new tournament scoring record, leading the field in driving distance at 323.1 yards and first in greens-in-regulation with 55 of 72) and the 2000 U.S. Open at Pebble Beach (where Woods would win by a record-breaking 15 strokes, finish as the only golfer under par and once again lead the field in driving distance at a hair under 300 yards and greens-in-regulation with 51 of 72) speak to his competitive muscle.

As a kid, Tiger's physical persona did not always match his competitive fire. Woods was tall and thin, with spindly legs, large glasses and an overbite. This image is a far cry from the million-dollar smile and powerful physique he sports today.

One night during those early days, while a student at Stanford University, Woods was returning to his dorm. A man with a knife jumped in front of him and demanded Woods' wallet, watch and a Buddhist symbol gold chain that was a gift from his mother. As the thief collected his haul, he turned the knife to its butt end and struck Woods in the face with it, causing Woods to fall to the ground as the thief made a quick exit.

Woods would require medical attention to attend to his wounds. When Woods' parents learned what happened, they were understandably concerned. When Woods finally had the opportunity to speak with his father, he told him, *"Pops, you know that overbite? Don't worry, it's gone now and my teeth are perfectly straight!"*

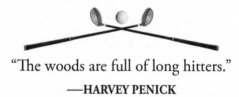

"The woods are full of long hitters."

**—HARVEY PENICK**

*"The object of golf is not just to win. It is to play like a gentleman, and win."* **—PHIL MICKELSON**

"Have you noticed that problems seem to compound themselves when we overreact to them? How often have you heard about a player slamming his putter after a missed putt only to have the shaft on the putter snap from the force of the impact? Now he has to finish out the round putting with his 3-wood. Problem's compounded. If our reactions surround us with negative energy, then the only thing we can possibly expect is negative consequences." —**MATTHEW E. ADAMS**

*"Winning golf is total commitment, physically and mentally. If you feel you are weak, you should be in the gym developing your body for golf."* —**NICK FALDO**

"Relax. Enjoy the walk between shots. That's you chance to loosen up so your next shot is comfortable." —**JULIUS BOROS**

*"Do your best, one shot at a time then move on. Remember that golf is just a game."* —**NANCY LOPEZ**

"Every shot counts. The three-foot putt is just as important as the 300-yard drive." —**HENRY COTTON**

*"It's 17 years of hard work and basically, the projections for my career 17 years ago weren't this nice."* —**JIM FURYK**, 2010 PGA Tour Player of the Year

"If your swing is good enough to win one out there, it's good enough to win again. Your problem isn't usually your swing. It's your heart." —**MARK MCCUMBER**

*"The most important shot in golf is the next one."* —**BEN HOGAN**

"Once you have gained an effective, repeatable swing, golf is played almost entirely between the ears."
—**SEVE BALLESTEROS**

*"Grip it and rip it."* —**JOHN DALY**

"Putting is always the great equalizer, because if you are putting well then it takes a lot of pressure off the rest of your game. You can afford to make a few mistakes if you're holing ten and fifteen-footers for par."
—**TOM WATSON**

*"When it's breezy, hit it easy."* —**DAVIS LOVE III**

"The average golfer, I can say flatly, lacks the ability to concentrate, which probably is the most important component of any good game. I believe the ability to concentrate is the difference in skill between the club player and the golf professional, even more than the shot-making process." —**DOW FINSTERWALD**

*"A golf swing is a collection of corrected mistakes."*
—**CAROL MANN**

"When hitting an approach putt, try to lay the ball into an imaginary three-foot circle around the hole."
—**BILLY CASPER**

*"Just controlling your breathing is I think an important thing out there. Just to try and slow your heartbeat down and walking a bit slower and just slowing your whole*

*rhythm down when you're getting down the stretch*
*or feeling a little nervous, just slow everything down*
*and try and relax."* —**ADAM SCOTT**

"I was struggling a little bit because I was starting
to fall in love with trying to make my swing more
technically correct on camera, with swinging the club
nice instead of effectively." ——**GRAEME MCDOWELL**

*"The golfer's left side must be the dominant part of the*
*swing. This is the only way to get maximum power and*
*accuracy. If the right side takes over, there is no golf swing."*
——**KATHY WHITWORTH**

"The ultimate judge of your swing is
the flight of the ball." ——**BEN HOGAN**

*"Concentration is not an element that should be applied*
*all the way around a golf course. It is not the least bit*
*important until you are ready to shoot. There's plenty of*
*time to concentrate when you step up to the ball."*
——**JULIUS BOROS**

"You've got to have an unbelievable short game.
You've got to hit your chip shots just perfect. It's not
like chipping out of a heavy rough. You've got
to putt really well, you've got to be precise with
your irons. You've got to drive it long and
straight now. And you've also got to think well."
——**PADRAIG HARRINGTON**, about the Masters

*"Never try a shot you haven't practiced."*
—**HARVEY PENICK**

"Everybody grips the club too tight, and in doing so, well, you think you have a lot more steam on it, but you don't. You don't get the speed that you do when you are nice and soft. I used to say, when I liked to go 300, maybe a little more and I'd just, nice and loose, and I said, 'Oh, Honey, I'm not going to hurt you. I'm going to take you nice and slow and easy.'"
—**SAM SNEAD**

*"Most fine putters are putters subconsciously. Putting is a psychology not a system."* —**MICKEY WRIGHT**

"Give it your best, but always with the realization that your happiness and your livelihood are not riding on the next shot." —**JANE BLALOCK**

*"Only fools live in the past."* —**CHI CHI RODRIGUEZ**

"You've just got to put yourself there; that's all you can do. You put yourself there enough times, you'll win."
—**TIGER WOODS**

*"The greatest single lesson to be learned from golf is mental discipline."* —**LOUISE SUGGS**

"Handling pressure is the difference between winning and losing." —**RAYMOND FLOYD**

*"You know, there are three clubs: Putter, driver, wedge. If you can master those three, you can win."* —**SAM SNEAD**

"You can't force wins. You have to take them one shot at a time." —**TIGER WOODS**

*"Sometimes the biggest problem is in your head."*
—**JACK NICKLAUS**

"If you believe you've prepared well, you've just got to get in and play, that's the bottom line. And obviously a self-belief you've got that you can finish it off. Obviously as the days increase and you've got to hit shots as the pressure mounts, you have to have a great self-belief, know that you can do it every time, a strong mental discipline, really."
—**NICK FALDO**

*"I'm a big hip player. I believe the hips are more so then the hands. The more I move my hips the better and straighter the ball flies."* —**DONALD TRUMP**

"Sometimes I wonder how the world would be if there were a million Johnny Millers. I guess some would disagree, but I think it would be a better place."
—**JOHNNY MILLER**

*"It sounds so simple but if you watch some of the best golfers in the world, it really involves keeping your head still and doing the same thing every time."*
—**SAM SAUNDERS**, about putting advice he received from his grandfather, Arnold Palmer

"Whatever you feel is not necessarily true."
—**TOM KITE**

*"Try to learn to drive your golf ball then work
on the rest of the game."* —**MILLER BARBER**

"The small things that happen in your life can
shape into bigger things." —**GRAEME MCDOWELL**

*"Sometimes if you're not good enough, you've got to
doff your cap and say you're not good enough.
It's a shame but that's the way it is."* —**LAURA DAVIES**

"Tom was a very mechanical player and I was more
of a feel player." —**BEN CRENSHAW**, about Tom Kite

## CHAPTER 13

# Light, Color and Space

## HOME FOR DINNER

Paddy O'Looney of Tralee, Ireland is somewhat of a golfing talisman. Blessed with the ability to make anyone feel at ease and as if they had known him all their lives, Paddy also possesses golf skills consummate with his diplomatic acumen (my father once told me that Irish diplomacy is "the ability to tell a man to go to hell, such that he looks forward to making the trip"). In keeping with his role as the St. Patrick of golf (Paddy heads up Swing Golf Ireland—www. SwingGolfIreland.com—a marketing consortium of multiple southwest Ireland golf courses), it is literally his job to spread the gospel of golf and the virtues of playing the game on the courses he represents, including the likes of Lahinch, Ballybunion, Waterville, Dooks, Tralee, Dingle, Ring of Kerry and Killarney, among others, collectively perhaps the finest assortment of courses anywhere in the world.

Over the years we have known each other, Paddy is always good to dispense some nugget of insight. Recently, he informed me that the men of County Kerry would preface a disparaging statement about another man, with the disclaimer, "in fairness" (another common form of this phrase, that sometimes provides more drama, would be "*in all fairness*," an even more encompassing sentiment, usually reserved for times when one is addressing a room full of people). For my apparent benefit (in order to ensure his message was idiot proof), Paddy proceeded to provide an example of this phrase's application: "In fairness, that Matty is not the sharpest @#%&ing knife in the drawer." While the message certainly hit it's target, the simple submission of in fairness provides the sense that some measure of equity was employed before another's character was assassinated, a sort of dispensation, if you will. I must admit that I have put such an allowance to good use on many occasions since Paddy's tutelage, in fairness.

One of Paddy's great life stories happened nearly fifty years ago, when he was but a strapping lad of fifteen.

It was commonplace that Paddy and his friends would play a minimum 36 holes a day at his home course, Partmarnock, north of Dublin and due to the sun setting after 11 pm at the height of summer, they could sometimes stretch that number to 54 or even 72 holes. The caveat being that if Paddy was going to be late for dinner, he had better let his mother, Vera, know of his tardiness in advance, lest she would be at home worried, a situation for which the golf rover would pay dearly when he would eventually return to the house. Vera's sentiment was acute at this time because less than a month before, her husband had passed away and while Paddy was also mourning his father's death, his presence around the house helped greatly to ease Vera's sorrow.

Even still a youth in his walk with the game, Paddy was already recognized as an emerging golfing talent and it was not uncommon that the better golfers at the course would seek him out for a game. Such was the case late one sunny summer afternoon after Paddy had played 36 holes with his friends and he was preparing to make his way home for dinner. "Paddy, lad, do you care to join us for a game?" came the siren call from none other than the legendary Irish golfer Harry Bradshaw. "If you can give me a lift home afterwards," Paddy negotiated as he was quick to ascend to the tee box, greeted by Harry and two other men, one smaller framed and the other rather stout (in fairness). He could not clearly make out their faces as the tee faced the Western sky and the descending sun silhouetted their form.

Tee shots are like personalities and they run the full lot. Such was the case on this day, as each party trotted off in varying angles to where their drives had come to rest and to prepare to hit their second shots. Striding up behind the smaller man just as he made contact with his ball, Paddy heard the man exclaim, "Oh, Uncle Bob would be impressed with that one," as his approach shot landed hole-high.

"This man's a bit long in the tooth to have an Uncle Bob," thought Paddy to himself, before turning to Harry Bradshaw, "Mr. Bradshaw, who is that man?"

"Bing Crosby," answered Bradshaw in a matter-of-fact delivery.

"Oh," said Paddy. "My mother loves him."

"His mother loves you, Bing," Bradshaw called out, to which the crooner allowed, "Thank God somebody does."

With that, they were off to play as many holes as the fading light would allow.

It was well past sunset by the time Paddy pointed out his house to Mr. Crosby, who brought the car to a stop in front of Paddy's door.

"Thank you for the ride, Mr. Crosby, it was a pleasure to meet you," said Paddy.

"Pleasure to meet you too, kid. Stick with the game, you're pretty good at it and tell your mom I'm sorry to have kept you out past suppertime." With that, Bing Crosby and Paddy O'Looney parted company.

Paddy danced through the door still tingling with excitement, but was instantly met with a cold front.

"Where have you been?" chided Vera.

"I've been golfing," replied Paddy with an air of entitlement that did little to appease his mother's discontent.

"With who?" demanded Vera, as Paddy knew she would—going straight for the bait.

"Harry Bradshaw…" Paddy revealed, pausing for dramatic effect before concluding, "… and Bing Crosby."

Now Vera was no fool and already aware of her son's rapidly-developing gifts for linguistics, she stood undaunted in her inquisition, even placing a hand upon hip.

"You'll have to do a lot better than that!" she exclaimed.

At this point, Paddy realized that his revelation of who he was playing golf with was not met with the instant dispensation he was expecting. Sliding to the kitchen table, Paddy took a seat and proceeded to tell his mother all of the details of the afternoon before. Slowly, her icy disposition was replaced with wonderment, especially upon learning that the great Bing Crosby had been only a few feet from her front door.

"Why didn't you invite him in for tea?" implored Vera.

"Because I wasn't sure you had your make up on," Paddy mumbled. Vera answered with silence, her disappointed eyes having spoke volumes.

Thirty years later, 84 year-old Vera O'Looney stood pressed against the rope line hoping to get a glimpse of Tiger Woods, a young golfer whose style and flash had captured her imagination. PGA Tour television coverage is an evening affair in Ireland (Ireland is five hours ahead of the East Coast of the U.S.A.), so the broadcasts usually come on the air between 7 to 9 p.m. GMT. Vera would never miss one, she was a complete pro golf junkie and while it still early in his career, with the tournament and Major victories he already had under his belt, Vera knew that in watching Woods she was witnessing the game's history.

Tiger had accompanied Mark O'Meara and a number of other pros and dignitaries to honor the memory of Payne Stewart at the Waterville Golf Links, where a statue of Payne was being dedicated. Payne Stewart loved Waterville, both the town and the Eddie Hackett designed layout. Stewart once maintained that he was so popular in Waterville, that he could easily be "elected mayor." Aside from introducing the Waterville golf course to his golfing buddies (they would make the sojourn prior to the

Open Championship to become acclimated to the time, weather and the links golf. It was a formula that was put to good use by Woods, O'Meara and David Duval—and most recently by Stewart Cink, prior to his 2009 Open Championship triumph), but Stewart would spend endless hours in the town's pubs, singing, playing music and just having a great time.

Paddy O'Looney was invited to the dedication ceremony by Jay Connolly, one of the owners of Waterville and Noel Cronin, Secretary/Manager of Waterville and one of the finest in the world at his craft. Paddy asked Jay and Noel if they would mind him inviting his mother to the special occasion, thus there she stood in awe of the golfing talent assembled before her.

By virtue of the status he had accrued in the world of golf, Paddy was one of the better-known representatives of the game in Ireland. He was already friendly with Mark O'Meara and when the opportunity presented itself, Paddy sided up to Mark and asked it he would mind introducing his mother to Tiger. "Of course, Paddy," the recent multiple-Major winner would agree and with that, Vera was introduced to the young golfer who had so captured her imagination.

By the time Paddy had made it back over to his mother, her face was still flushed from all of the excitement.

"I guess this makes up for Bing," grinned Paddy to his mother, a debt paid some three decades on. Vera could only manage a smile and nod of confirmation, her eyes twinkling in appreciation.

"A great golf course both frees and challenges a golfer's mind." —TOM WATSON

*"A golf course is alive, literally. They grow, settle, and evolve. They are constantly changing. The rest of the world is also changing all the time, and it will happen whether we wish to be a part of it or not. We must embrace change to grow, learn, and advance, or we die."* —**MATTHEW E. ADAMS**

"If I put my name on something, I am committed to it. Golf courses are like a fingerprint of life. You build a golf course and in 200 years it is still going to be here. I'm going to be dead and buried, but my name and design are going to continue on… that's the most important part." —**GREG NORMAN**

*"It gets better, I think. I don't know whether it was a tram or a train or whatever, but we came by the golf course and I'm looking at it, it's all trodden down. There's sand with a few this and that and the other on it. I look over on the course and I thought, 'Gee, they must still be using sheep over here. That has not had a machine on it.' I asked the guys if this was a disbanded course and the guy jumped up and said, 'I'll have you know, that's St. Andrew's.' Yeah, he was really hot. Each time I played that course, I respected it more and more and more. It was something else."*
—**SAM SNEAD**, 2001 interview

"In my opinion, the architects have ruined the game. They all want to be Picasso." —**LEE TREVINO**

*"I feel like I have an eye for design work."*
—**JUSTIN LEONARD**

"I saw a golf course that was a revelation to me. Very much different from the golf that I knew at the time. I was amazed at the way they dressed at the course." —**BEN CRENSHAW**

*"To see where the tours go now is really mind blowing."*
—**PETER JACOBSEN**

"A golf course is to me holy ground. I feel God in the trees, and the grass and flowers, and in the rabbits and the birds and the squirrels; in the sky and the water. I feel that I am home."
—**HARVEY PENICK**, from *A Game for a Lifetime*

*"You can talk strategy all you want, but what really matters is resiliency."* —**HALE IRWIN**

"Ben Hogan said that putting and the game of golf are actually two different games. The game of golf is played in the air, and putting is played on the ground. How democratic, then, is putting! You need not be the strongest, fastest, or best-equipped, to challenge those who may be your superior in all other areas." —**MATTHEW E. ADAMS**

*"You've got to have the guts to get it done. You can have a picture perfect swing or you can have a range swing that looks great; you can put the club in every position. But can you pull the trigger when you have a 3-iron over water*

*on the last hole and need to make 3? Can you do it? Well,*
*that's when it comes down to what do you have inside."*
**—TIGER WOODS**

"The mind messes up more shots than the body."
**—TOMMY BOLT**

*"Management, placing the ball in the right position for*
*the next shot, is eighty percent of winning golf."*
**—BEN HOGAN**

"In addition to preparing the mind, you must prepare
the muscles for a round of golf. The average golfer
claims he hasn't the time to warm up, when the truth
is he won't make or take the time. A four-hour round
of golf can certainly be preceded by ten or fifteen
minutes on the practice tee. By simply hitting a dozen
balls you have eliminated three or four bad holes
from your system. If you won't hit practice shots,
at least swing something heavy before driving off."
**—JACKIE BURKE JR.**

*"Never have a club in your bag that you are afraid to hit."*
**—TOM KITE**

"To make that 10-footer or 5-footer
really takes a lot of focus." **—ERNIE ELS**

*"When you're out there on the golf course and
the wind starts blowing, you have to hit certain shots.
You may not have an opening in the trees, you've got
to hit this one. Practice these shots, don't be so limited
in what your mind creates."* —**TIGER WOODS**

"Take your lies as they come. Take the bad bounces
with the good ones." —**BEN CRENSHAW**

*"Don't analyze your own swing. The chances are you can't
do it properly. Have a pro do the job."* —**SAM SNEAD**

"Practice is the only golf advice that is good
for everybody." —**ARNOLD PALMER**

*"Practice is not to take the place of teaching, but to make
teaching worthwhile."* —**HARVEY PENICK**

"Grip-it-and-rip-it's always there. I just don't have
to try and hit it past these guys. My goal is just to
play good around the greens and that's where you
win." —**JOHN DALY**, on playing against younger golfers

*"Focus not on the commotion around you, but on the
opportunity ahead of you."* —**ARNOLD PALMER**

"The difference between winning and losing is
always a mental one." —**PETER THOMPSON**

*"Fear of any kind is the number-one enemy of all golfers,
regardless of ball-striking and shot-making capabilities."*
—**JACK NICKLAUS**

## CHAPTER 14

# The Right Weight

## JACKLIN'S WORDS OF WISDOM

The career of Tony Jacklin has been compared to that of a streaking comet; brief, yet brilliant. Jacklin was born into a working class family in England and at one time was an apprentice steelworker. His father introduced him to golf at an early age and by the time he was in his early teens he was winning tournaments. At 17 he turned professional. Scratching and clawing his way through the ranks, in 1969 he won the Open Championship, the first Englishman to win since 1951, and in 1970 he posted a seven-shot victory at the U.S. Open, the first Brit to win the event since 1920.

Jacklin's triumphs revitalized the game in his native land. Jacklin was a seven-time team member of the Ryder Cup (his was the putt famously conceded by Jack Nicklaus in 1969 to end the matches in a

**149**

halve) and he is unquestionably one of the cornerstones of the success of the European Ryder Cup team, having captained the team in 1983, 1985 (the Brits'/Euros' first victory since 1957), 1987 (first Euro win on American soil) and in 1989.

Jacklin's distinctive career also earned him the honors of the Order of the British Empire and the Commander of the British Empire.

Recently, Jacklin recounted to me a source of inspiration that he carried throughout his career. It was a simple poem, given to him by a friend who used to caddy for him. Jacklin's friend has long since passed, but his words, and inspiration, live on. Here is the text of that poem:

> *"If you think you are beaten, you are.*
> *If you think you dare not, you don't.*
> *If you would like to win but think you can't, it's almost certain you won't.*
> *If you think you'll lose, you've lost.*
> *For out in the world, you'll find, success begins in the fellow's will.*
> *It's all in a state of mind.*
> *Think big and your deeds will grow.*
> *Think small and you'll fall behind.*
> *Think that you can and you will.*
> *It's all in a state of mind.*
> *Life's battles won't always go to the strong or fast at hand, but sooner or later, the man who wins is the man who thinks he can."*

"Match your strategy to your skills."
**—ARNOLD PALMER**

*"…a golfer may at any time hit that one spectacular shot just as well as Ben Hogan, Arnold Palmer, or Greg Norman. Just the chance to do that is what keeps bringing them back."* —**PETE DYE**

"I expect to hit at least five bad shots."

—**WALTER HAGEN**, on expecting adversity

*"The game of golf allowed me to pursue other interests. Careful scheduling allowed me to focus on different things. Balance is very important to me. Thankfully, I have the ability to concentrate on one task at a time, devote the necessary time to that project and then turn the page and concentrate on what's next."* —**GREG NORMAN**

"Desire, dedication, determination, concentration and the will to win." —**PATTY BERG**, on being a champion

*"The golf history books are long on stories of how a match was decided not on the merits of who had a better swing or mastery of the fundamentals of golf, but simply because one of the competitors defeated himself through the complete loss of composure and concentration."* —**MATTHEW E. ADAMS**

"Ask yourself how many shots you would have saved if you never lost your temper, never got down on yourself, always developed a strategy before you hit, and always played within your capabilities." —**JACK NICKLAUS**

*"Do not be tempted to invest in a sample of each new golfing invention as soon as it makes its appearance. If you do you will only complicate and spoil your game and encumber your locker with much useless rubbish. Of course some new inventions are good, but it is usually best to wait a little while to see whether any considerable section of the golfing public approves of them before rushing to order one."* —**HARRY VARDON**, 1908

"All professional golfers owe a debt of gratitude to Walter Hagen, for he was the man that opened the door of status to the generations of golfers who followed. His personality demanded that he be at the center of the clubhouse cocktail party rather than simply toiling in the golf shop or changing his shoes in the car." —**MATTHEW E. ADAMS**

*"He fought the hook, just like I did, for 25 years, and I don't know anything tougher than fighting a hook. He eliminated the hook from his game, that's how he became such a great player."* —**TOMMY BOLT**, about Ben Hogan

"I never hit a shot, not even in practice, without having a very sharp, in-focus picture of it in my head. It's like a color movie." —**JACK NICKLAUS**

*"I had enough good shots that week and some good solid putts at the right time and that's what got me through."*
—**BEN CRENSHAW** on winning his second Masters title

"Never concede the putt that beats you."
—**HARRY VARDON**

*"Know your strengths and take advantage of them."*
—**GREG NORMAN**

"Play golf to the hilt. Win, lose, or draw, good day or bad, you'll be happier for it, and you'll live longer."
—**ARNOLD PALMER**

*"There was never a shot that I didn't think I could play."*
—**ARNOLD PALMER**

"There's an old saying, 'It's a poor craftsman who blames his tools.' It's usually the player who misses those three-footers, not the putter."
—**KATHY WHITWORTH**

*"I've worked really hard for this. I've had ups and downs through my whole career but it's worth the work. It's just amazing."* —**MICHAEL CAMPBELL**

"When you play St Andrews and there is not a lot of wind, that putter is the one stick that is going to win you the golf tournament." —**TOM WATSON**

*"If you can just stick to your guns and keep working hard, it'll turn around. And it really did turn around for me in the second half of last year. I won in Sweden and a few weeks later I won over here. So if you just keep with the plan that you've got, I think it can always turn around."*
—**ADAM SCOTT**

"You just rely on those memories sometimes to pull yourself out of it that you've done this before even in the worst circumstances and you've turned it around. There's no reason why you can't hang in there and turn this around as well." —**TIGER WOODS**

*"When you're playing well you can raise your game to another level when you have to."* —**DAVID TOMS**

"I always looked at The Open over here as a championship that was very different. I enjoyed the break. I enjoyed the difference in the golf. I enjoyed the different kind of golf, the seaside golf. It was something that was not my normal forte that and I learned to adapt my game to it, rather than you hear a lot of players say, 'I can't play that course.' That's a bunch of junk. A good player can play any course. You adapt your game to the golf course. You don't adapt the course to your game." —**JACK NICKLAUS**

*"Many shots are spoiled at the last instant by efforts to add a few more yards."* —**BOBBY JONES**

"Majors are always amazing and you always look forward to coming back and playing. You know, they are tough and everybody says so but, you know, I always look forward to playing those. You know, it's what we work for and what we practice for. So it should be fun." —**SERGIO GARCIA**

*"They don't give out the winner's check on Thursday, they give it out on Sunday. So to me it's trying to get myself prepped for that sprint to the finish on Sunday and hopefully hang in there until then."* —**HALE IRWIN**

"Great champions have an enormous sense of pride. The people who excel are those who are driven to show the world, and prove to themselves, just how good they are." —**NANCY LOPEZ**

*"You hear that winning breeds winning, but no, winners are bred from losing. They learn that they don't like it."*
—**TOM WATSON**

"At the end of the day, it is only a golf tournament."
—**ROBERT KARLSSON**

*"It was humbling. It gives you a lot of hope that we are good people, even though there are some strange characters out there and some not so nice people, there are some absolutely fantastic people out there."* —**KEN GREEN**

"You get on a roll like that and you think, why can't I do that every week?" —**CRAIG STADLER**

*"It's just good competition, it makes everyone better."*
—**TONY JACKLIN**

"You got to stay ahead of the game."
—**ZACH JOHNSON**

*"Getting your first win is always a big step in confidence."*
—TOM KITE

"I have a good feeling about this and that's all I'm gonna say. It was a historical feeling. For some reason I knew that place was going to take care of us."
—BEN CRENSHAW, regarding his feelings on the eve of the singles matches at the 1999 Ryder Cup

*"I think in golf there's ways to win without winning the golf tournament. It's about making progress. I think when a guy qualifies for the Tour that's a win, when you make enough money to make the top 125, that's a win."* —LARRY RINKER

"It was a very unprofessional stroke, that's why they have winners and losers." —HUBERT GREEN, on losing the Masters

*"I tried to only get mad at myself but I was plenty mad at myself plenty, plenty of times."* —BEN CRENSHAW

"I have been lost so many times." —BEN CRENSHAW

*"Those players that are there, I assure you they feel the pressure. They feel that stuff and that's what they play for."*
—HALE IRWIN, on Ryder Cup pressure

## CHAPTER 15

# An Exercise of Intellect

## A Recipe for Success

I t is always fascinating to pick the brains of successful people. The funny thing is, there is great conformity in their essential approach to winning. While their particular dishes may vary, their methods provide a kind of recipe for success, if you will.

Here are some of the basic ingredients to success that I have perceived from the great champions.

1. **Outwork your competition**. There will always be someone bigger, stronger, faster, smarter and better connected, but nothing can beat the merits of hard work. Do not ever let someone out work you.

2. **Know who you are**. Recognize your strengths, but also know your weaknesses so that you can work to overcome them. Contrary to most amateur golfers, champions spend the most time practicing the parts of their games in which they are the weakest.

3. **Never Give Up.** Even when the world has given up on you, a victory is often just past the line where everyone else has dropped out of the race.

4. **Have a plan.** Champions use road maps. They have a specified approach for each element of their game, from their season, career, practice routine, each round of golf and each individual shot. Know what you want to do, do not leave it to chance.

5. **Believe you are the best in the world**. ALL champion golfers believe they are the best. ALL of them. If you believe for one second that you cannot beat another golfer, then you won't. Champions have a belief in themselves they use as their armor in the battle.

6. **Practice positive.** Champions do not dwell on negativity. Think about how many amateur golfers you know that constantly denigrate their game ("I'm the worst putter in the world," "I stink at this game," etc.). Can you imagine sitting down with a surgeon, asking him about his experience and he replies, "Actually, I'm the worst surgeon in the world!" (reference Rule # 5, above). If you want to be the best, you

have to believe yourself capable of it (then seek out help to get there and work like crazy).

In conclusion, it is no coincidence that I believe that golf is a metaphor for life. Wouldn't our chances for success off the golf course also benefit from the wisdom of the champions?

As we've been shown by the great chefs of success, if one follows the recipe, even augmenting it with his own particular flair, then success can be replicated.

"I personally don't feel like I'm 50 years old, but I've done a very good job of making sure I don't feel older than what I am. I feel like I'm in my low 40s to tell you the truth, and I'll stack up myself against a lot of guys fitness wise, and I think that's what the secret is. Keep yourself mentally solid, physically strong, and you can pretty much do whatever you want to do." —**GREG NORMAN**, on turning 50

*"It is something that I'm still coming to terms with. But since I've become No. 1 I've finished second, third and first. So, I think I can cope with it."* —**LEE WESTWOOD**, on being the World # 1 Ranked Player

"Don't play too much golf. Two rounds a day are plenty." —**HARRY VARDON**

*"Most golfers lament their fates to forces beyond them, however, the existence of this 'victim mentality' is not exclusive to the golf world. In fact, it is so prevalent in our society that it is nearly at epidemic levels. Perhaps in an effort toward preservation of one's self-image, it is easier to blame the bad things that have happened to us on twists of fate, not accept them as results of some action we took or failed to take. It is simply a question of accountability. Great champions accept accountability if not for more noble reasons then for the simple reason that if we feel completely at the whim of circumstances that we cannot control, then how can we possibly compete? Not only are we competing against an opponent, but we are also subject to the fickle injustices of millions of other variables."*

—MATTHEW E. ADAMS

"I can't get better as a player if I don't get better as a person." —TIGER WOODS, 2010

*"Don't give advice unless you are asked."* —AMY ALCOTT

"Fear comes in two packages, fear of failure, and sometimes fear of success." —TOM KITE

*"That's why the majors are so hard, because they test you to the limit."* —VIJAY SINGH

"Golf is a matter of confidence. If you think you cannot do it, there is no chance you will."

—HENRY COTTON

*"I stop thinking at 8 in the morning when I get up."*
—**FRED COUPLES**

"Worry is poison." —**PETER THOMSON**

*"You are what you think you are, in golf and in life."*
—**RAYMOND FLOYD**

"The year after I started golfing I think I won half the
events on the surfing tour. That it planted seeds in
my head was the biggest thing that golf did for me."
—**KELLY SLATER**, world champion surfer

*"Seve [Ballesteros] is at home watching this because
he can't be with us right now. Every player out there knew
what he meant to European golf. We know what this means
to him. We brought this trophy back. It's a special day."*
—**IAN POULTER**, 2010 Ryder Cup

"When Tiger Woods was a kid, he had Jack
Nicklaus' impressive achievements taped to his wall
as motivation. Even for a golf prodigy like Woods,
Nicklaus' golfing accomplishments read like something
superhuman that only a fool or someone severely
self-deluded would even aspire to. But Tiger Woods
was different. He did not use Nicklaus' record as an
opportunity to take account of his deficiencies, but as a
road map to success—as a cause of self-empowerment,
not resignation." —**MATTHEW E. ADAMS**

*"I've put myself in so many different scenarios and have been successful and have failed, and I've had to learn from both. Why did I fail? Well, because of this. Why did I succeed? Well, because of this. You have to analyze, you have to be critical and you have to understand that you have to take hard looks at yourself."* —**TIGER WOODS**

"I thought 50-year-olds were pretty old when I was 30. Or your parents are 50, you think, 'How can anybody be that old?' But now that I'm 50, you really don't think about what you were thinking about when you were 30. I haven't grown up any. I'm still 30. I may feel 50 or 60. But inside, I'm still 30."

—**MARK CALCAVECCHIA**

*"In choosing a partner, always pick the optimist."*
—**TONY LEMA**

"It is important that we continue to remind ourselves that we are winners. Winners use failure as a building block to improve and learn, to get stronger."
—**MATTHEW E. ADAMS**

*"Discipline and concentration are a matter of being interested."* —**TOM KITE**

"I thought of Padraig Harrington. I thought of Zach Johnson, Y.E. Yang and Lucas Glover, Trevor Immelman, all these guys who won majors for the first time. I thought, 'They could do it, so can I.'"
—**GRAEME MCDOWELL**

*"There is no doubt that confidence is built through success, but it can also be built through having the courage to try the very thing that all around you would advise against."*
—**MATTHEW E. ADAMS**

"You mature through failure, not success."
—**JERRY PATE**

*"I learned early that whatever I got out of life, I'd have to go out and get for myself."* —**WALTER HAGEN**

"It's not that I don't watch golf because I don't enjoy the game. I don't watch golf because I'm not a spectator. Never have been a spectator in any sport."
—**JACK NICKLAUS**

*"If I ever say I'm tired of signing (autographs), someone please club me over the head with a 9-iron."*
—**PADRAIG HARRINGTON**

"To be a golfer is to be an optimist, for we all believe that our next round will be better than our last."
—**MATTHEW E. ADAMS**

*"There are only two things you can do with you head down, play golf and pray."* —**LEE TREVINO**

"If he was any more laid back he'd be horizontal."
—**GRAEME MCDOWELL**, about Angel Cabrera

*"We've been through a lot in the last year. To win this, it's very emotional—very special and very emotional."*
—**PHIL MICKELSON**, 2010 Masters

"I can only control what I can do." —**TIGER WOODS**

*"I kind of look at birdies like deposits in the bank. You can never have too many deposits because you're always going to have withdrawals."* —**FRED FUNK**

"We create success or failure on the course primarily by out thoughts." —**GARY PLAYER**

*"The healing road is up and down."* —**KEN GREEN**

"I am very proud of my year. All the goals I set for myself happened; to win the Race to Dubai, to play in and win the Ryder Cup and to win a Major."
—**MARTIN KAYMER**, 2010 PGA Champion

*"You've got to figure out what works best for you. That's the hard part. I know I can't play as stoic as Hogan, and I can't talk as much as Trevino; you have to be your own person."*
—**TIGER WOODS**

"He said, 'Dad, show me. Show me you can still play this golf course.' You know what? I wanted to show him I can still play the golf course."
—**TOM WATSON**, after a 67 in first round of 2010 Masters

*"The greatest gift your parents can give you is choices, and that comes from the highest education you can get."*
—**LEE TREVINO**

"I think I was always the same person, I just had a different outlook on where my future was."
—**JERRY PATE**

*"I think you could ask yourself questions like that all the time. What if I practiced longer hours? What if I worked out four days a week? What if this? I mean, there are what-ifs every day in this game. I think that's the nature of this game."* —**DAVID TOMS**

"I'll look back at my life and say what could have been. If this is the worst thing that happens to me ... I am not going to have a pity party."
—**KENNY PERRY**, after losing in playoff, 2009 Masters

*"I probably learned more in the last 12 months than I did in the first 10 years of being a professional. I feel like I might have wised up a bit. Struggling a little bit last year will certainly help me in the long run."* —**ADAM SCOTT**

"It's like life. You have your ups and downs a little bit and you've got to keep working on the right stuff and surround yourself with good people that will help you out and just keep working hard. It's never as far off as you think." —**HUNTER MAHAN**

*"Because playing my own game is good enough to beat pretty much everybody. That's my fatal flaw, if I have one, is I try too hard sometimes."* —**CRISTIE KERR**

## CHAPTER 16

# The Long View

## IN CELEBRATION OF THE BOLD

Y ou heard the outcry didn't you? Heard the electronic snickering, the printed ridicule and the worldwide golf-media mocking?

The March 2008 edition of *Golf World U.K.* (not affiliated with the U.S. version of the magazine by the same name) featured a long article about eccentric English professional Ian Poulter.

Poulter is best know for his hairstyle that approximates the look of the Sunday rough at the U.S. Open, and a wardrobe defined by a kaleidoscope of brilliant colors not otherwise known in the physical world (interesting then, that Poulter posed sans cloths in the publication, thankfully sparing the populace any more intimate knowledge through the strategic placement of his golf bag). The article was, to say the least, revealing.

In the interview, Poulter is quoted as saying, "The trouble is I don't rate anyone else…I really respect every professional golfer, but I know I haven't played to my full potential and when that happens, it will be just me and Tiger." He continued, "It would be a dream to see Tiger Woods and then me in the world rankings as you look down. What's wrong with that? Is it being rude? Is it being disrespectful to everybody else? I don't think so."

With the predictable precision of Big Ben, the world golf media pounced on Poulter's comments like a lion on a gazelle. *"Who does he think he is?"* was the most common response from the global scribes. *"How dare he challenge Tiger Woods and discount all others in the process?"* was the paraphrased response (remember, at this time, Tiger was still in the middle of what would be a five and a half year run as the # 1 ranked golfer in the world and it didn't appear that his reign at the top was going to end any time soon).

Why, the 32-year-old Poulter had won as many majors at that time as Tiger Woods had won *Dancing with the Stars* crowns. Exactly none.

So it came as a shocking bit of hubris to the sentries of all things golf-proper that this veteran golf professional who seemed to have mastered nothing more than a distinctive look as comparison to the mountain of accomplishments of Tiger to that point, should publicly put himself in the company of Woods. So intense, in fact, was the media lambasting that Poulter released a statement noting, "The whole answer to the question has been taken out of context," and therefore, warped its true meaning (few of the news agencies that picked up the original story related that Poulter stressed, "Tiger is one in a million. Actually, Tiger is one in 10 million. He is extraordinary. If you look at the rankings he is almost two and a half times better than the guy in second place [Phil Mickelson])."

The entire affair was not lost on the World No. 1, mind you. When trudging through his post-round interviews after yet another start, and win, this time at the Dubai Desert Classic (with Poulter in the field), Woods was asked a question about the significance of the space between he and the No. 2 golfer in the world. Woods answered incredulously, joking to the reporter, "I thought Ian Poulter was No. 2?"

The assembled media and the broadcast's hosts all yukked it up as Woods bore his way through the masses, basking in the glow of another stunning victory and leaving yet another upstart seemingly foolish enough to openly voice his aspirations, reduced to dust, both figuratively and in reality. This is the world of professional sports. One would be foolish to believe that a competitor would reach out to another and help them up the ladder.

Trying to place all this into perspective, I initiated an internet search for reactions to those who have been bold enough to verbally challenge Woods' position as the best golfer on the planet. The initial quote results were eye opening, to say the least. Here is a sampling of some of the responses:

*"You'll learn."*

*"…[he] is not bigger than the game."*

*"…well, he's a rookie. He'll learn. You've got to play by the rules [of what is expected of you]."*

*"This tournament was one of seven to help him out at the beginning with sponsor exemptions when he needed help, and how quickly he forgot [after withdrawing the day before the first round]."*

*"How he goes about scoring from where he hits it—that's the amazing thing."*

What's really amazing was that these comments were not about upstarts and wannabes; rather, my search criteria must have had a mind of its own, for these comments were *about* Tiger Woods himself.

What? Who would be foolish enough to pull on Superman's cape, you say?

Well, by order of comment, the first was said by Curtis Strange in response to a cub Tiger pronouncing that his goal was to "win every time out." The next pearl came from Hal Sutton in 2001, explaining his mental posture prior to winning the Players Championship (the full quote is even more impressive, Sutton having said, "Tiger Woods is not bigger than the game. The other night I was lying in bed and I said, 'You know what? I'm not praying to him. He's human just like I am'").

None other than Davis Love III uttered the next statement when asked to react to Woods' last-minute decision to pull out of the Buick Challenge in his rookie year. In fact, the statement about "…how quickly he forgot" was also by Curtis Strange reacting to the same withdrawal as Love. The last statement was by Stephen Ames on the eve of his 2006 Accenture Match Play Championship match against Woods (which an inspired Woods went on to win by a crushing score of 9 and 8).

Woods, of course, is famous for his ability to channel such comments into laser-like intensity; feeding off what he perceives as a slight into crystal clear focus on the field of battle.

"It's different. It's not physical, where you can go up there and put a shoulder in somebody and take them out. It's not like that. It's about the ability to bear down and pull out quality golf shots on your own, and you go put an inordinate amount of pressure on your opponent," explained Woods.

Aside from the risks inherent in challenging Woods in a verbal arena, there is another observation that the passage of time allows us. While most of us can feel quite smug about ridiculing anyone who states their intention to challenge Woods, I wonder how many people remember when it was Woods himself who was mocked and ridiculed for his "win every time out," or his "Hello World," press conference as a wet-behind-the-ears TOUR newbie? Well, 14 Majors later, who's laughing now?

Remember Colin Montgomerie's press conference after the second round of the 1997 Masters when he suggested that with his experience (and Woods' lack of it) in Majors, that he would be better able to handle the pressure? The next day, Woods shot a 65 to Monty's 74, leaving the veteran to comment after the round, "Let me tell you this. Tiger Woods is going to win this event...there is no chance...we're all human beings here, no chance humanly possible that Tiger Woods is going to lose this tournament." Woods, of course, went on to win by 12 shots.

Reflecting on Montgomerie's comments after the tournament gave some insight into Woods mentality. "He basically said I didn't have much of a chance because of my experience level. But I was playing well.

I said to Fluff (Woods' caddy at that time), 'He may have said all those things, but he hadn't won a major, either."

Remember when Rory Sabbatini, the oft-maligned, if misunderstood Tour player, boldly stated, "I want Tiger…everyone wants Tiger."

As history has proven, such a brazen pronouncement did not turn out all that well, as Woods overtook Sabbatini in the third round of that year's Wachovia to earn yet another victory. However, Sabbatini's post-tournament observations had anything but a conciliatory tone. "The funny thing is, after watching him play last Sunday, I think he's more beatable than ever," he said. "I think there's a few fortuitous occasions out there (translate: luck) that really changed the round for him at Wachovia. And realizing that gives me even more confidence to go in and play with him on Sunday again."

More recently, a young Australian named Jason Day announced that when Woods looks into his rear view mirror, it may be Day that he sees closing in. "He has so much time. He played 16 events, what does he do with his time? He'd be aware of me. He'd be saying, 'Here's another kid coming up,'" said Day when asked if he thought Woods knew who he was.

Smelling the sensational scent of a brewing story line, the media sought out Day at Pebble Beach prior to the start of the tournament (Day would finish the event in sixth place) and asked the 20-year-old for more on his objective to overtake Woods.

"Obviously, Tiger Woods is the No. 1 right now; he's the benchmark. Whether it takes me five years or 20 years, I would like to hopefully one day achieve that spot. I'm still going to work hard. Tiger is Tiger and you can't deny that. He is the greatest golfer. I respect Tiger so much. He's changed my life in more ways than anyone could have foreseen (this latter comment was in reference to Tiger Woods being Day's inspiration to turn his life around after some wayward years following the death of Day's father, from cancer, when Day was only 12 years old)."

Recently, Phil Mickelson, who cannot escape comparisons to Woods, even if he wanted to, was asked to size up his ability to come out on the winning end of this year's Majors with Woods standing in his way. Mickelson, clearly sensing the danger of wading into such treacherous waters answered with the deft touch of a political aspirant when he explained that if anyone beats Woods, "I hope it is me."

Having noted the sometimes detrimental results of those golfers who were bold enough to challenge Tiger at the height of his dominance, I love the fact that some professional golfers have the intestinal fortitude to do it (for haven't we all found ourselves complaining that golfers play it too safe, never really saying what is on their mind, always striving to avoid controversy and say the right things?). However ill advised it may have been at the time, isn't it refreshing to hear an unvarnished opinion? Shouldn't we strive to celebrate such honesty instead of treating it with scorn?

Tiger Woods' march into the record books has given us a chance to watch the making of history right before our eyes, however, I don't think we need to buy into a collective thinking that no one else can ever challenge Woods at his best or any of the other best golfers of the world today, including Lee Westwood, Phil Mickelson, Jim Furyk, Rory McIlroy, Graeme McDowell, or even, yes, Ian Poulter. What's more, do we want a core of golfers behind the top who simply collapse and are intimidated before they reach the first tee?

However delusional we may feel another's visions of grandeur are, big thinking should be celebrated. Critics (and media) owe it to the game and to the fans to not simply become part of a larger marketing machine. Wouldn't the fact that it was once widely proclaimed that no one could ever challenge the record of Jack Nicklaus be evidence enough that nothing lasts forever?

The next time a professional golfer is honest enough to state for the record that he intends to dethrone the current king, maybe we should use the lessons of history itself to realize that someday, someone is going to back up the bravado with performance.

It is quite clear that we live in a world of resignation, and those persons with high aspirations are greeted with the unsolicited coaching of *"you'll learn to lower your expectations."*

Isn't the first step to becoming a champion about having the conviction that you are capable of doing it, even when the world thinks you are crazy?

Just ask Tiger.

"To be a champion, you must act like one."
—**HENRY COTTON**, 1934, 1937 and 1948 Open Champion

*"Everyone knows in their heart whether or not they have given it their all, whether they prepared their best, and whether they have been totally committed to every shot."*
—**TOM LEHMAN**

"To win, you must treat a pressure situation as an opportunity to succeed, not an opportunity to fail."
**—GARDNER DICKINSON**

*"Professional golfers need to maintain mental road maps of what they wish to accomplish in a tournament, season, or career. They need to know what aspects of their games they can most count on when the pressure is on, and they need to be honest about where the weaknesses are in their games so that they can work to minimize them. They also need to set goals to measure success or failure in these areas…*

*On the golf course or off, we all need a clear picture of what our game plans are. Where is it that we want to end up? How do we get there? Unfortunately, most of us have no game plan, or map for getting where we want to go. How do you know where you will end up when you have no route to get there?"*—**MATTHEW E. ADAMS**

"Great players learn that they don't need to play their best golf to win. They only need to shoot their lowest score." —**TOM WATSON**

*"An Open [Championship] is not really only a measure of how you handle a golf course, it is a measure of how you handle yourself, how patient you are, how experienced you are."*
**—JACK NICKLAUS**

"The point is that it doesn't matter if you look like a beast before or after the hit, as long as you look like a beauty at the moment of impact."

—SEVE BALLESTEROS

*"Every shot in golf should be played as a shot at some clearly defined target. All players realize this…But what many of them forget is the shot off the tee should also be aimed at the target down the fairway."* —CRAIG WOOD

"Once you have a game plan, in golf or in life, it serves as an internal compass to keep you on the path to achieving anything you want regardless of what the competition throws at you." —MATTHEW E. ADAMS

*"I didn't win in the 1930s because I hadn't yet learned to concentrate, to ignore the gallery and the other golfers, and to shut my mind against everything but my own game."*

—BEN HOGAN

"I never wanted to be a millionaire. I just wanted to live like one." —WALTER HAGEN

*"I'll probably play 25 or 26 events around the world. If I can win 25 or 26, it will be a good year."* —TIGER WOODS

"Winning takes care of money titles. It takes care of Player of the Year awards. Ultimately what you want to do is win championships and major championships. Hopefully my 30's can be more productive than my 20's and I can win more major championships." —**TIGER WOODS**

*"Be decisive. A wrong decision is generally less disastrous than indecision."* —**BERNHARD LANGER**

"If I had it to do over again, I wouldn't beat myself up so much." —**GARDNER DICKINSON**

*"I'm not really concerned about what my legacy is in relation to the game of golf, frankly. I'm more concerned about what my legacy is with my family, my kids and my grandkids. That's by far more important to me. If I've done it properly out here and I can hold my head up to my kids and grandkids, that's the most important thing."*
—**JACK NICKLAUS**

"All of golf's great champions believed themselves capable of doing big things. It was their ability to think big that gave them the confidence and conviction to win, over and over again. Thinking big helps us to see a world of opportunity that may have previously been just outside our range of sight. It allows us to look at the possibilities on the horizon without having our view obscured by perceived obstacles that stand between us and our wildest dreams. Thinking big is not only fun; it is critical to success." —**MATTHEW E. ADAMS**

*"It is nothing new or original to say that golf is played one stroke at a time. But it took me many years to realize it."*
—**BOBBY JONES**

"You create your own luck by the way you play. There is no such luck as bad luck. Fate has nothing to do with success or failure, because that is a negative philosophy that indicts one's confidence, and I'll have no part of it." —**GREG NORMAN**

*"Concentration comes out of a combination of confidence and hunger."* —**ARNOLD PALMER**

"Don't be too proud to take lessons." —**JACK NICKLAUS**

*"It's a young world. I see them all as competitors. I love the position I'm in. I would love to stay there. And to do that I have got to work hard and set new goals and push myself hard to get better. It's a combination of everything, but I'm so competitive. I'll do anything to beat them all, really. That's my goal."* —**ANNIKA SORENSTAM**

"I don't want to look backward. I want to look ahead and look at myself and improve what I can improve in my golf game. That is one thing that I have control of. I love to come out and compete and that is why I am here." —**ANNIKA SORENSTAM**

*"I am going to continue to get better that is my goal. I want to continue to win tournaments. I welcome every challenge, I always have. I am not going to give it away too easily. I love the position I am in and I love what I do."*
—ANNIKA SORENSTAM

"Columbus went around the world in 1492. That isn't a lot of strokes when you consider the course."
—LEE TREVINO

*"It's not whether you win or lose, but whether I win or lose."*
—SANDY LYLE

"Sometimes the most fun golf shots are those that carry the greatest risk; those that defy logic with their tiny percentage of likely success. Those that take big thinking to conceive and an iron nerve to execute…
Thinking big is a developed trait. We can train ourselves to embrace the possibilities without giving in to limiting self-doubt. The chief inhibitor to thinking big, to going for it, is fear. Fear of failure. Fear of rejection. Fear of ridicule for trying something over our heads. Often, you are the only one who knows what your potential really is. The challenge is to have the courage to follow your conviction and embrace the possibilities regardless of internal or external pressure to settle for less."
—MATTHEW E. ADAMS

*"Just keep playing better, just keep improving and keep getting consistency on my game, improve my short game and hopefully get a little better with my putting. And, you know, I think if I do that and I keep that consistency that I had last year on my long game, I think that, you know, I could do some nice things. I'm just going to go one step at a time and try to play the best I can every week and try to do the best I can every week."* —SERGIO GARCIA

"I definitely improved, not only in my game, but the way I approach the game, how I take things on the golf course. That's also important. It's not only maturing as a player, but also knowing what's going on around the golf course, how to take all those good and bad things." —SERGIO GARCIA

*"To be honest, 50 now isn't 50 ten years ago. I would say 50 now is 45, maybe even close to 40 from 15 years ago. Just with better health, better conditioning, just everything is better. People are younger now at 50 than they were. If that makes sense."* —SAM TORRANCE

"Well, the implements we used were more difficult to handle, I'll put it that way; it wasn't more brain work. I don't think the human brain has developed any further than it was 50 years ago. We're stuck with the same worries and cares and prejudices and things like that...So everything that's happened in the development of the game has actually taken away some of the chance that was there in golf. One of the great things about our game is the element of chance, it's pretty big, as games go. And I hope it will always remain so." —**PETER THOMSON**

*"40 is just a number I think in my mind. I'm physically much stronger now than I was when I was probably 25. You know, I never did any weights. The experience I have now, the physical ability I have, I should be able to, you know, maintain or even progress in my ability. I'm not slowing down working out. I'm working out the same as I did last year. You know, I feel really good. I feel free from injury, just looking forward to having a good season, not to worry about too many other factors."* —**VIJAY SINGH**

"You know, I really feel like I've just got to get better, keep improving and let my clubs do the talking."
—**SERGIO GARCIA**

## CHAPTER 17

# Don't Give Up!

## ONE FOR THE AGES—THE MIRACLE OF '86

There really wasn't much reason for optimism. Jack Nicklaus, after all, was 46 years old. And this was The Masters. Jack hadn't won a tournament in two years, hadn't won a major in six years. It had been nine years since he had played as many as 16 tournaments in one year.

So, there really was no reason to think that in 1986, Jack Nicklaus would be able to do what everyone considered "impossible." He was, in his own words, "an old guy out there playing golf who wasn't supposed to compete anymore."

Jack himself could understand the public's general perception. It had been "five years", he said, since he really, truly cared about being a touring professional golfer. By the time he was 46, he was heavily into his course design business, he was getting into the golf club business and he had a number of outside interests to occupy his time. He was the proud father of five grown children and a very active wife. In short, he wasn't Jack Nicklaus who was totally into competing at golf. He was now Jack Nicklaus, the man who was more into family and business than he was at winning golf tournaments. He had his time, and it was brilliant, by any account.

"I really wasn't working at it that hard," admitted Jack. "Did I try to prepare? Sure. But I didn't prepare to the extent that I did when I was right in the middle. I just didn't have any motivation to move in that direction."

It was against that backdrop that Nicklaus went to Augusta in '86. With him for the first time ever in his professional career was his mother. And he did care greatly about Augusta, where he had won five times. He loved the course and the club over-all, and this was one tournament that he prepared for like no other.

In playing seven tournaments leading into Augusta in '86, Nicklaus had missed the cut three times, withdrew from another event and didn't have a finish higher than 39th.

The late Tom McCollister was a golf writer in Atlanta at the time, and a friend of Nicklaus. He had handicapped the field early in week, giving his choices for the eventual winner. His opinion of Jack's chances, however, wasn't good. He cast Jack as a 100-to-1 shot, saying his pal was "washed up."

A friend of Nicklaus spotted the story and taped it to the refrigerator in the house in which Jack was staying. It was in a very prominent position, front and center on the refrigerator door. Every time Jack went to the fridge, he was certain to have a look at the article. It was, Nicklaus admitted, "a little extra motivation."

What wasn't generally known that year, by McCollister or anyone else, was that Jack actually had putted very well early that year. He had stumbled onto a large-faced putter, one the press immediately dubbed the "omelet pan." The putter was destined to become famous by Sunday night.

"I hadn't really hit the ball that well, I hadn't really done very much golf-wise," he said. "I don't know, I'd won a grand total of a couple thousand dollars or something, maybe a couple hundred dollars. I don't even know what I'd won, but anyway it wasn't very much.

"And I got to Augusta and I started hitting the ball better. Augusta always sort of inspired me. I always went in the week before. I always prepared myself and always got ready for the golf tournament and I did the same thing that I normally do to try to get ready. I enjoyed that—it was always fun for me to do so."

The tournament began and Nicklaus didn't do much. He shot 74, which was six shots worse than the leaders. McCollister's prediction appeared to be coming true. No one, it seemed, cared what Jack might or might not accomplish the remainder of the week.

Thursday evening, Nicklaus was depressed because, "I played pretty well but I didn't make any putts, I didn't putt very well." He found reason for optimism, however, because his putting hadn't been a problem all spring—the problem had been his ball striking. And now his ball striking was pure. If he could find his putting touch again, then there was at least some hope for the last three rounds.

And sure enough, Jack went out Friday and shot a 71, then followed that on Saturday with a 69. He still wasn't anyone's choice to add a sixth green jacket, not with Seve Ballesteros, Greg Norman, Nick Faldo, Tom Kite, Tom Watson, and Bernhard Langer in the field, and all looking like potential champions. But Nicklaus was getting a little attention now because this 46-year-old man was looking like he might have a chance to finish in the top 10. He had climbed all the way to the eighth position, just four shots out of the lead.

Sunday morning Jack received a call from his son, Steve. In the course of conversation, Steve asked, "What do you think it will take, Pops?"

"I think 65 will win the tournament," said Nicklaus. "I think 66 will put me in a playoff." Son Steve said, "Exact number I had in mind. Just go shoot it."

Jack didn't do much to shoot a 65 the first eight holes. He had a bogey and a birdie and was even par for the day. On No. 9, though, he was preparing to putt a 12-footer for birdie when he heard a big roar from No. 8, then almost immediately heard another from the same area, then another as the players had all hit magnificent shots. Jack turned to his playing partner, Sandy Lyle, and with a grin said, "Hey, why don't we see if can make a little noise ourselves?"

Then he poured in the putt, the first of several as he set out on his famous march to another green jacket.

"Not that it made any difference at that point because I was still 10 miles behind," said Nicklaus. "But I holed a 25-footer at the next hole (No. 10) and 25-footer at the next hole (No. 11). And I said, 'That's pretty exciting. Now I'm nervous.' You know, why would I be nervous?

I mean I'm not even anywhere near it, but I'm nervous because I think I can get into contention."

Jack woke up to reality a bit at No. 12, the short par-3, when he missed a 6-foot par putt and made bogey. But wonder of wonders, that bogey might have eventually meant the championship. "It might have—it put me back—brought me back to the reality that, you know, that I have got to still play golf," said Nicklaus.

Number 13 is a par-5, and with a good drive and 3-iron, he hit the green in two shots and made another birdie—his fourth in five holes. Jack parred 14, but on the par-5 15th it was time for yet another series of heroic shots.

"I hit a really nice drive—put it in the right position on the fairway," he remembered. "And I turned to Jackie (his son, Jack Jr., was his caddy that day) and I said, 'How far do you think a three will go here?'"

Nicklaus meant a '3' on the scorecard. He had glanced over the leaderboard, where Kite, Norman, Ballesteros and Watson were battling furiously to squeeze out an advantage. And Jackie knew exactly what Nicklaus meant.

"He said, "I think it will go a long way, Pops."

"So I just took dead aim on it and it never left the pin. And then it started to trickle down to the left about 12 feet." He had covered the 240-yard distance with a 4-iron, his adrenalin was riding so high. And then he strode up to the ball, bent over in his famous crouching stance, and stroked it into the cup for an eagle.

Could it be? Well, could it? At last, Nicklaus knew that he was right in the heart of contention.

"Now I'm pumped," Nicklaus said. "I know I'm just a couple of shots behind at that point."

Now came 16, and this wasn't Jack Nicklaus, occasional golfer and fulltime businessman. This was Jack Nicklaus circa 1964, when his whole focus was what happened on the golf course. And at 16, he swung a 5-iron from 175 yards and heard Jackie say, "Be right." The reply from Jack—"It is."

"It was one of those times where I hit the shot and as soon as it left the club, I knew exactly where it was," he said. "It was just sort of a cocky remark that I made. I don't normally make that. But I had so much confidence in what was going on, that's what I did."

The ball landed 12 feet from the hole. Jack studied the putt closely.

"You know, it is not as easy a putt as it looked because I had a little putt that was sort of—it wasn't dead straight forward, it was a little putt that would break backwards in front of the green. So I had to take it inside the left edge. And I made the putt, obviously, and the place went wild."

So Nicklaus walked to the 17th, and heard another huge rumble from the crowd. Ballesteros, playing at 15, had knocked his approach into the water. Seve took a bogey, and suddenly Nicklaus had the lead—though at the time he didn't realize it.

Jack half-wanted to cry, half-wanted to shout. "I saw (Ballesteros) out in the fairway and I knew he'd hit it in the water," said Nicklaus. "And I hate that sound because half of the cheering is for me, which I don't like when somebody makes a mistake, and the other half was the groan for (Ballesteros), who hit it in the water."

But on the other hand, Nicklaus was pumped up by the crowd, energized because suddenly a lot of old emotions came flooding back.

"You know, it's kind of fun to go to a place and have it be wild again," said Jack. "It had kind of been a few years since I'd seen any of that."

A drive and a wedge from 110 yards put him just 12 feet from the flag at 17. "I looked at Jackie and he said, 'Dad, it's got to go right,'" recalled Nicklaus Senior. "I said, 'I know it's going to go right, Jack,' but I said, 'I think it's going to come back left at the hole.'"

The putt did exactly as he thought—for yet another bird. Now Nicklaus knew exactly where he stood, knew he had the lead by himself. Up ahead of him was the final hole, and a perfect drive left him 175 yards to the flag.

Unfortunately, just as he swung his 5-iron, he felt a gust of wind hit him in the face, and he knew that wasn't good news. The ball dropped 40 feet below the pin. But here Jack had another secret weapon—intimate local knowledge of the green, since his architectural company had redone this green during the summer of '85.

He knew the putt would be faster than it once was, but it wouldn't have the extreme break of years past. He stroked it with these thoughts in his mind, and it was a perfect lag putt. One more tap-in, and Nicklaus had completed the back nine in 30 strokes for a final round 65. Sixty-five, exactly the number he had predicted to Steve in the morning phone call.

Nicklaus had done all he could. Now there was a matter of a 45-minute wait in the Jones Cabin while Norman and Kite each had chances to tie him.

The best chance came from Norman who had made four consecutive birdies beginning at the14th hole. As he played the 18th hole, he had tied Jack for the lead. Norman hit his approach from the middle of the fairway, a 4-iron, but alas, he blocked it into the crowd. He could only make bogey, and 46-year-old Jack Nicklaus was the champion.

It was quite possibly his most-watched win ever, with television cameras joining the live crowd which was trumpeting his every move for 2 ½ hours. And even today, Jack admits he gets tingles when he watches the old film of the Miracle of '86.

"It was just the end of a great week," he says. "It was not only fun, but it was something really neat to think that, you know, here I've come back. And I hadn't worked out. I'd been playing 12 tournaments a year, going through the motions.

"It was kind of a neat week, a neat thing to go through. It was great for me because it felt like I actually had done something well."

Of all of his accomplishments and victories never did Jack win as meaningful a title as the 1986 Masters.

"Resolve never to quit, never to give up, no matter what the situation."—**JACK NICKLAUS**

*"So for me right now, golf is secondary. My family is primary because I spent so much time away from them for 25, 30 years. Then comes business because I really do love business because that's going to be my back nine. I'm not going to be playing golf when I'm 65. I really want the last ten years to take place where I can have a wonderful business career and choices to make in the next five or ten years."*

—**GREG NORMAN**

"I don't know if you're ever finished trying to improve. As soon as you feel like you are finished, then I guess you are finished, because you already put a limit on your ability and what you can attain. I don't think that is right." —**TIGER WOODS**

*"I don't really feel like I could ever give back to this game and the people involved what it's given to me, but I'd like to at least start chipping away at that, because it's blessed me more than I could have ever dreamed."* —**DAVID DUVAL**

"It's a mystery to me, that I continue to do this well, especially at my age…My passion for golf, my passion for life, is what keeps me young." —**DANA QUIGLEY**, 2005 Champions Tour Player of the Year

*"No matter what happens, never give up a hole. In tossing in your cards after a bad beginning, you also undermine your whole game, because to quit between the tee and green is more habit forming than drinking a highball before breakfast."* —**SAM SNEAD**

"Win graciously." —**ARNOLD PALMER**

*"If you're serious about improving your play, be brutally honest with yourself."* —**GREG NORMAN**

"One of the last conversations I had with Payne Stewart was at the Ryder Cup a few months before his passing, actually just a few weeks, and in that conversation he talked to me about his concern for the future of the game and whether we were doing enough to use the way our veteran players handle themselves to instill in our younger players the understanding of what is important about the game and what needs to be perpetuated for those that follow. That is what continuing of the traditions of the game is all about." **—TIM FINCHEM**

*"Believe me; I'm going to be involved in golf until the day I die from whatever angle I can be involved in it."*
**—PETER JACOBSEN**

"Sometimes you lose your desire through the years. Any golfer goes through that. When you play golf for a living, like anything in life, you are never going to be constantly at the top." **—TOM WATSON**

*"What's past is past and the only future to me is the first tee shot tomorrow and go from there. That's the way I've always approached it. Simplistic and boring, but that's the way it is."*
**—HALE IRWIN**

"When you've got kids it's easy to sit there and say that everything's perfect, but if you fast forward 50 years and it's not the same as we have it, it's not fair. If we have control over that then I just want my kids to have the same opportunities I had and if I can do anything to help it, that's a great thing."
**—GEOFF OGILVY**, on recycling

*"There has got to be a massive move with parents and children and schools, educating people and children about Mother Earth."* —**GARY PLAYER**

"We do it for the love of the game."
—**LEE TREVINO**, on continuing to play in tournaments

*"We've got to put all our efforts into the young people. They are our future. What are our great grand children going to inherit?"* —**GARY PLAYER**

"I'm turning 60 years old very quickly and I don't know how good I am going to be yet." —**TOM KITE**

*"If you prepare properly in life for the things you want to accomplish, if you are patient and don't get too anxious, I think you'll truly find that there's a lot of quality that comes out of that whole thing."* —**DAVE ADAMONIS, SR.**

"When my game goes and I'm not competitive, I will hang them up, but still play for a few dollars against my friends." —**RAYMOND FLOYD**

*"The main thing is that I was able to play a game I loved and continue to love. It has so many facets about it other than playing golf. I've been lucky enough to travel and see so many different parts of the world."* —**BEN CRENSHAW**

"There are so many more things I want to do, perhaps I don't need to do them but I want to do them."
—**HALE IRWIN**

*"He's a remarkable kid. He's unbelievable the way he plays golf. He out drives them, he out putts them, he out thinks them. He's got a better short game than they have. He gets it up-and-down from anywhere. You can't put him out there anywhere that he can't get it up-and-down. We've already seen that. It's unbelievable how good he is, unless something serious happened or unless somebody gets hot and shoots some good rounds, he's going to be unbeatable."*
—**TOMMY BOLT**, about Tiger Woods

"Wind and rain are great challenges. They separate the real golfers. Let the seas pound against the shore, let the rain pour." —**TOM WATSON**

*"One might as well attempt to describe the smoothness of the wind as to paint a clear picture of his complete swing."*
—**GRANTLAND RICE**, on Bobby Jones

"Sam Snead is one of a handful of golfers who inspire the club players with the conviction that golf is easy."
—**PETER DOBEREINER**

*"The game of golf has taught me the value of perseverance and imagination, of having a game plan and knowing who you are. It has revealed to me more than a lifetime's worth of its universal truths."* —**ARNOLD PALMER**
from the Foreword from *Fairways of Life*

"Yeah, I like the golf courses really tough."
—**RETIEF GOOSEN**

*"It's hard not to play golf that's up to Jack Nicklaus
standards when you are Jack Nicklaus."*
**—JACK NICKLAUS**

"I think I was given a gift to play golf and
to be mentally strong." **—KARRIE WEBB**

*"I have come to understand and appreciate writers much
more recently since I started working on a book last fall.
Before that, I thought golf writers got up every
morning, played a round of golf, had lunch, showed up
for our last three holes and then went to dinner."*
**—PHIL MICKELSON**

"Aggressive play is a vital asset of the world's greatest
golfers. However, it's even more important to the
average player. Attack this game in a bold, confident,
and determined way, and you'll make a giant leap
toward realizing your full potential as a player."
**—GREG NORMAN**

*"Success in golf depends less on strength of body then upon
strength of mind and character."* **—ARNOLD PALMER**

"I used to get out there and have a thousand swing
thoughts. Now I try not to have any." **—DAVIS LOVE III**

*"Sarazen, Palmer, Nicklaus, and Woods were among
the greats who were criticized in their youthful debuts
on Tour for being 'over confident or too brash.' Yet their*

*belief in their ability had more to do with setting high goals for themselves, versus looking down on their more seasoned competition. They were all big thinkers. Big thinkers do not prequalify themselves as being too small, too inexperienced, too young, too late or not ready. They take the chance without reservation. They let everyone else convince themselves that they are not ready for the challenge, thus diminishing the competitive field.
Big thinkers are busy looking forward while everyone else is looking backward. They define their self-image by what they will be, not what they are, or have been. Detractors dismiss them as 'dreamers.' In fact, dreamers are exactly what they are. They know that if you do not have the courage to dream big then you will never accomplish big things."* —**MATTHEW E. ADAMS**

## CHAPTER 18

# Good-bye, For Now...

## FINDING A PATH

The reputation for the tenacity of Ben Hogan and his laser-like focus has taken on almost mystic proportions. History illustrates that Hogan won 64 times on Tour (4th all time) and that he won nine Major championships, placing him in a tie for 4th on the all time list of Majors won, along side of Gary Player. Hogan's Majors were as follows:

> Masters Tournament: 1951, 1953
>
> U.S. Open: 1948, 1950, 1951, 1953
>
> Open Championship: 1953
>
> PGA Championship: 1946, 1948

As distinctive as are his Major championships is the knowledge that he won six of his nine Majors after his horrific car accident of 1949 that nearly took his life and required him to limit the amount of golf he played due to pain in his legs (effectively making Hogan the first golfer who geared his limited schedule around golf's biggest events). In 1953, Hogan won three of the four Majors he entered (he did not play in the PGA that year as it was still at a time when the PGA's dates would float and Hogan could not play due to a scheduling conflict). Hogan also was among the first golfers to take copious notes on every hole he played. Hogan firmly believed that course management, placing the ball in the correct position for the *next* shot was the most important thing a golfer could do to ensure the best chance to score. While Hogan is not credited with the origins of using the modern Yardage Book (that credit generally goes to Jack Nicklaus), a strong argument could be made that it all started with Hogan.

Hogan also competed on two U.S. Ryder Cups teams, in 1947 and 1951 and he captained the team three times, 1947 (playing Captain), 1949 and 1967.

Hogan's awards and distinctions are too numerous to list, but the highlights include winning the Vardon Trophy for the lowest scoring average in 1940, 1941 and in 1948 (a year in which he won 10 times); leading money winner in 1940, 1941, 1942, 1946 and 1948; and PGA Player of the Year in 1948, 1950, 1951 and 1953.

Hogan was also among the inaugural class of the World Golf Hall of Fame in 1974, he won the Bob Jones Award, the highest honor of the United States Golf Association in 1976 and more recently, Hogan was ranked 38th in ESPN's "SportsCentury: 50 Greatest Athletes of the 20th Century."

Against this mountain of accomplishment, it's unfathomable to realize that even the great "Hawk" had to fight his way through self-doubt. In both 1932 and 1933, he tried and failed to make a living as a touring professional, but he soldiered on. In 1935, after Hogan married the former Valerie Fox, she traveled with him. The height of Hogan's despair reached a critical point in 1938. At one point, the Hogan's stripped an orange tree of it's fruit, virtually living off their haul for weeks. While contending deep into a tournament at the Claremont Country Club, during the California swing, Hogan's spirit was nearly broken. Emerging from his hotel the morning of the final round, Hogan was shocked to find his Buick jalopy up on blocks, the two back tires having been stolen. Prior to this tournament, Hogan had promised Valerie that if he had not found a path to success as a professional golfer by this tournament, then he would hang up the clubs and "never mention golf" to her again. Hogan was in a desperate state, having no money to fix his car, much less provide sustenance for Valerie and him moving forward (the Hogans needed to make $150 per week just to cover expenses).

However, Hogan is a legend for good reason. Rather than resign himself to inexplicable fate, Hogan ironically hitched a ride with Byron Nelson to the tournament and played like a man possessed with desperate purpose. Hogan would post a final round 67, and earn $285, enough to afford tires and drive to the next tournament in Sacramento. There, his good form continued and he came away with a check for $350. By the end of 1938, Hogan would finish 13th on the money list with $4,794 in earnings.

It is quite plausible to point to this event as the moment when Hogan became the golfer of the legend he is known as today. Hogan himself would call 1938 his "turning point."

Funny how sometimes it is the very pinnacle of one's frustrations; literally, the razor's edge of giving up is the bridge that divides success and failure.

"To me, my record is 18 professional majors, five kids, 46 years of marriage, 19 grandkids and a successful business. I have other friends, I have enjoyed what I have done, and I have been able to smell the flowers along the way. Those are the things that are important to me, not the 18 majors. The 18 majors are not my life, they are part of it. If I had been really serious about building a record that nobody was going to touch, I wouldn't have been able to do a lot of the other things I have enjoyed. I have had a very balanced life. I spend time with my kids, I have grown up knowing them, and if golf had been the only thing I did, that wouldn't have happened. I could have won 20 or 25 majors, but I think I would have been a miserable person."
—**JACK NICKLAUS**, July, 2006

*"I would like to leave the game better than when I found it."* —**ARNOLD PALMER**

"It was nice to get to go home and sleep in your own bed. You just lie there and think, 'Oh, my goodness, U.S. Open champion.' It's crazy."
**—PAULA CREAMER**

*"I feel great. Never felt better in my life. You've got to keep enthusiastic and you've got to keep happy if you want to live a long time."* **—GARY PLAYER**, at age 70

"If I had to cram all my tournament experience into one sentence, I would say, 'Don't give up and don't let up!'" **—TONY LEMA**

*"It's been the best week of my life."*
**—RORY MCILROY**, after 2010 Ryder Cup

"Keep your sense of humor. There's enough stress in the rest of your life to let bad shots ruin a game you're supposed to enjoy." **—AMY ALCOTT**

*"This is my moment."* **—LEE WESTWOOD**

"Always keep it fun. If you don't have fun, you'll never grow as a person or a player." **—TIGER WOODS**

*"I remember when my dad was 50. I thought he was old. I asked my kids, 'Is 50 old?' They said, 'Well, yeah, mom, but you don't act 50.'"* **—JULI INKSTER**

"He reminded me of me when I was 18."
**—TOM WATSON**, about Ryo Ishikawa

*"It's the Holy Grail for us. If you don't believe in God, that's fine with me, but you're going to believe in some sort of God, because this place is absolutely breathtaking."*
—**BILLY ANDRADE**, about Pebble Beach

"The first thing anybody has to do to be any good at anything is believe in himself." —**GAY BREWER**

*"I should have kept myself in better shape, which is still the case. I should have won more tournaments. I should have practiced harder—a lot of should haves. On the other hand, I had a great time ... I stop to think about all the things that I've been blessed with, and I just had a blast."*
—**MARK CALCAVECCHIA**

"Sometimes the fastest way to reach our major goals is to realize we have nothing to lose in making the effort."
—**MATTHEW E. ADAMS**

*"Never tell yourself you can't make a shot. Remember, we are what we think we are."* —**GARY PLAYER**

"Play golf to the hilt. Win, lose, or draw, good day or bad, you'll be happier for it, and you'll live longer."
—**ARNOLD PALMER**

*"I said this was going to define my career, but you know what, it made my career."* —**KENNY PERRY**, 2008 Ryder Cup

"Don't hurry, don't worry. You are only here for a short visit. So don't forget to stop and smell the roses."
—**WALTER HAGEN**

*"And I'll go away from this game thinking, well,
I've been highly successful at something I wanted to be at."*
**—COLIN MONTGOMERIE**

"The place I'm going someday soon will be better than any golf course or winning any championship, because I'm racing for a prize that will last forever."
**—BYRON NELSON**, in 2006 at age 94

*"I miss the people, I miss the enjoyment of seeing their smiles and shaking their hands."* **—LEE TREVINO**

"The reality of it is, if you don't believe it, I can absolutely prove it to you. The more I've given in life, the more I received and when you put your life in that point, when you give first and don't expect anything in return and keep giving, good things happen to you and I've always believed it but I didn't practice it until I had a little tragedy in my life; and you get low enough in the barrel and thank God I didn't lose a life, a limb, a job, or a family member, or a wife. You know there's lots of losses you experience in life. I lost some things that weren't as important as other losses that other people have lost, and at the same time I've had enough education and experience to be able to go out and help people and try to help people work through their problems, 'cause life is about people working together and trying to do for one another and when we get that way in the world, the world is pretty peaceful and successful, but when we get into selfishness, greed, and all about me and my ego and money, then we have all this chaos around the world and it can be as chaotic in the locker room about competition as it can be in the Middle East." —**JERRY PATE**, on rebuilding his life after injury derailed his playing career

*"I have a zestful life. The most important word in your life is love, and the love you get from your family is imperative."* —**GARY PLAYER**

"Learning to compete is one of the great joys of life." —**TONY JACKLIN**

*"At some point I'll sit down and reflect on what's been a life-changing season. It's been a whirlwind ride, and it's been certainly something I'll be trying to reflect on and enjoy."* —**GRAEME MCDOWELL**, 2010

"I'm just enjoying 'late life' and it's pretty neat." —**RAYMOND FLOYD**

*"No. I'll never mature. I'll be a kid until I'm dead."* —**MARK CALCAVECCHIA**

"If we preserve the integrity of golf as left to us by our forefathers, it's up to all of us to carry on the true spirit of the game." —**BEN CRENSHAW**

*"If this is the worst it's going to get, I'll be a very happy man."* —**PADRAIG HARRINGTON**, on a winless 2010 season

"I think I'm still climbing. Yes, I've been there but those are just several peaks in the mountain range."
—**HALE IRWIN**

*"This ... is the greatest moment of my golfing career."*
—**COLIN MONTGOMERIE**, 2010 European Ryder Cup Captain

"It's been a great ride.
I've enjoyed every moment of it." —**JERRY PATE**

*"I felt at peace. I really felt very content. I walked up to hit my third shot on the 18th, and I felt the breeze coming in, and it was just a really comfortable feeling. I saw some players standing behind the 18th green, that gave me a tear. I saw my parents and my family and that gave me a tear."* —**ANNIKA SORENSTAM**, on retirement

"I wish I had the words of Winston Churchill to say the appropriate thing. You'll go to your grave knowing you had tremendous love showered upon yourself." —**GARY PLAYER**

# ABOUT THE AUTHOR

**M**ATTHEW E. "MATT" ADAMS is an international golf travel reviewer, *New York Times* best-selling golf author, PGA Tour Network broadcaster and golf commentator, and regular contributor to the Golf Channel, in addition to multiple media outlets throughout the world, including ESPN and the BBC.

Matt has written ten books, two of which became New York Times best sellers. He also is an award-winning international golf broadcaster where he hosts the daily program, *Fairways of Life*.

*Fairways of Life* is a golf lifestyle show that focuses on luxury golf travel, golf equipment and the game's history. Matt's guests have included Jack Nicklaus, Arnold Palmer, Gary Player, Tiger Woods and Greg Norman. His show is heard throughout North America on the PGA Tour Network, on Sirius and XM Satellite Radio and around the globe on PGATour.com.

Adams travels internationally and he frequently reviews golf in Ireland, where he is a recognized expert. In 2010, Paddy O'Looney,

CEO of SWING Golf Ireland declared Adams the "Golf Ambassador to Ireland."

He also runs a golf consulting company and has done live play-by-play for the PGA Tour and the Champions Tour. He is an expert on equipment technology and golf history. He worked at ESPN before joining a golf-equipment manufacturer.

Matt is a member of the Golf Writers Association of America, International Network of Golf, Press4Golf (U.K.), National Association of Sportswriters and Sportscasters, Shivas Irons Society, Club Managers Association and Ancient Order of Hibernians.

Matt is a highly sought-after professional speaker, delivering inspiring stories of triumph. To contact Matt's office or schedule him for your next event, please visit www.FairwaysofLife.com.

# FAIRWAYS OF LIFE

For an even deeper Fairways of Life experience, be sure to log onto
www.FairwaysofLife.com for a free newsletter!

Also, be sure to listen to the *Fairways of Life* show each weekday
from 7 to 9 a.m., on the **PGA Tour Network, Sirius XM Radio**
(in North America)

Twitter: **Twitter.com/MattAdamsFoL**

To book Matthew Adams to speak at your corporate
or charity event, log onto www.FairwaysofLife.com
and click on "Contact"

# BUY A SHARE OF THE FUTURE IN YOUR COMMUNITY

These certificates make great holiday, graduation and birthday gifts that can be personalized with the recipient's name. The cost of one S.H.A.R.E. or one square foot is $54.17. The personalized certificate is suitable for framing and will state the number of shares purchased and the amount of each share, as well as the recipient's name. The home that you participate in "building" will last for many years and will continue to grow in value.

**Here is a sample SHARE certificate:**

## YES, I WOULD LIKE TO HELP!

*I support the work that Habitat for Humanity does and I want to be part of the excitement! As a donor, I will receive periodic updates on your construction activities but, more importantly, I know my gift will help a family in our community realize the dream of homeownership. **I would like to SHARE in your efforts against substandard housing in my community!** (Please print below)*

PLEASE SEND ME _____ SHARES at $54.17 EACH = $ $_____

*In Honor Of:* _____

*Occasion: (Circle One)*    *HOLIDAY*    *BIRTHDAY*    *ANNIVERSARY*

     *OTHER:* _____

*Address of Recipient:* _____

*Gift From:* _____ *Donor Address:* _____

*Donor Email:* _____

I AM ENCLOSING A CHECK FOR $ $_____ PAYABLE TO HABITAT FOR HUMANITY **OR** PLEASE CHARGE MY VISA OR MASTERCARD *(CIRCLE ONE)*

Card Number _____ Expiration Date: _____

Name as it appears on Credit Card _____ Charge Amount $ _____

Signature _____

Billing Address _____

Telephone # Day _____ Eve _____

**PLEASE NOTE:** Your contribution is tax-deductible to the fullest extent allowed by law.
**Habitat for Humanity • P.O. Box 1443 • Newport News, VA 23601 • 757-596-5553**
**www.HelpHabitatforHumanity.org**

Printed in the USA
CPSIA information can be obtained
at www.ICGtesting.com
JSHW082201140824
68134JS00014B/370

9 781600 378652